Legal Aspects of Technology Utilization

Legal Aspects of Technology Utilization

Richard I. Miller
Harbridge House, Inc.

Lexington Books
D.C. Heath and Company
Lexington, Massachusetts
Toronto   London

Library of Congress Cataloging in Publication Data

Miller, Richard I
    Legal aspects of technology utilization.

    1. Intellectual property—United States. 2. Patent laws and legislation—United States. I. Title.
KF2979.M5   346'.73'048   74-16943
ISBN 0-669-96172-8

Published simultaneously in Canada.

Printed in the United States of America.

International Standard Book Number: 0-669-96172-8

Library of Congress Catalog Card Number: 74-16943

Contents

List of Figures

List of Tables

Table of Cases

Use of the Carterfone Device in Message Toll Telephone
Service, 13 F.C.C. 2d 420

Water Services, Inc. v. Tesco Chemicals, Inc.,
410 F. 2d 163

Preface

What is happening in the law of intellectual property to affect the utilization of innovation in high technology? In 1973 the National Science Foundation commissioned the multinational management consulting firm of Harbridge House, Inc., to find out. The project staff of four lawyers, led by the author, borrowed their hypothesis from the biological sciences. As the littoral between the earth and the seas frequently reveals the developing pattern of life on the land and in the water, so too developments in the law may be usefully traced by examining cases and controversies that do not fit neatly into the established legal disciplines. In this instance, the lawyers examined the gray areas between patent and antitrust, patent and trade secret, and trade secret and copyright to disclose the influence of the law on the behavior of businessmen involved in the utilization of technological innovation.

Appreciation is gratefully extended to the professional project staff: Frederick J. Hopengarten, Francis J. Kelley, and Paul F. Richards; to Michael Bergner, the project director of the 1968 Government Patent Policy Study, on whose shoulders we all stood; to the support personnel, Deborah C. Notman, Suzanne Endemann, and JoAnn Elliot; to the Patent, Trademark and Copyright Research Foundation of the Franklin Pierce Law Center; to the Association of Data Processing Service Organizations; and to the many individuals and organizations in industry, education, and government whose time and talent made this work possible.

Part I
The Concept

Just the place for a Snark! I have said it twice:
That alone should encourage the crew.
Just the place for a Snark! I have said it thrice:
What I tell you three times is true . . .

—Lewis Carroll, "The Hunting of the Snark"

1

Study Objectives

The objectives of this study of the Legal Incentives and Barriers to Utilizing Technological Innovation grew, in large part, out of the findings of an earlier Harbridge House study. In 1968 Harbridge House submitted a voluminous report to the Committee on Government Patent Policy relative to operations of the Statement of Government Patent Policy issued by the President in October 1963. The government patent policy study was directed to three fundamental policy issues:

1. What effect does patent policy have on industry participation in government research and development programs?
2. What effect does patent policy have on the commercial utilization of government-sponsored inventions?
3. What effect does patent policy have on business competition in commercial markets?

The findings of the study provided the foundation for a revised Memorandum and Statement of Government Patent Policy issued by the President on August 23, 1971. The principal thrust of the revisions was to mandate changes designed to increase the commercial utilization of government-sponsored research. The next step was the publication of regulations by departments in the executive branch complementing the presidential memorandum.

The effectiveness of the policy changes cannot be properly evaluated until the departmental regulations have been operative for at least several years. This study, therefore, does not pretend to be an evaluation of the revised governmental patent policy. It is, however, a sequel to the earlier work and expands upon the conceptual theme. Though broader in scope in some dimensions, it is narrower in others; in all respects, limitation of resources has restricted the findings of this study to a more modest data base.

A nagging problem that permeated the government patent policy study was the constant reminder that *patents*, although the star of the show, are not the whole show. The law of intellectual property includes more than patents. Government policy includes more than patents. Commercial practice includes more than patents. Why, then, was the earlier study—and, indeed, are most government studies—restricted to patents? For one thing, a good patent does, in fact, provide the strongest possible protection under the law for technological innovation. For another, patent analyses are quantifiable. The number of

3

applications filed and patents issued each year is a matter of public record. Finally, Congress has preempted patent law; thus developments in patent law are relatively easy to follow. On the other hand, the other members of the legal family that comprise the law of intellectual property are rooted in common law and are subject to state as well as federal jurisdiction. Consequently, they are somewhat more scattered. But they are there. They are significant. It is idle to presume that the effect of government policy regarding intellectual property can be measured by patents alone.[1]

Although the legal concepts under consideration in this study include the entire body of the law of intellectual property, the scope of inquiry has been narrowed. It is here concerned solely with commercial utilization, and not merely the commercial utilization of government-sponsored inventions, but with all technological utilization. It is not primarily concerned with industrial participation in research and development programs, nor in the effect of government policy on business competition. Yet all of these problems are so interrelated that a concentration on one aspect of the commercial utilization inquiry necessarily involves some comment about the others.

By the same token, the law of intellectual property cannot be totally isolated from the larger body of commercial, tax, and regulatory law which impacts upon the commercial development of technological innovation. All of the law has an influence on commercial development at all times. The most that can be pinpointed is that some bodies of law appear to exercise a greater influence at a given stage of development than others in the long journey a technical innovation takes in becoming an accepted commercial product or modification of such a product.

Considering innovation and market development as a continuous, interactive process, rather than regarding the former as an isolated exercise of intellect, a cycle may be projected which starts with research and includes mileposts of experimental development and market introduction on the way to a product which is accepted in commercial markets. Market acceptance invites a continuous process of product modification and improvement (hence, back to research) in order to maintain, expand, and, if possible, dominate the market.

In the early stages, the significant legal disciplines tend to be protective. The familiar cluster of protective disciplines identified with the law of intellectual property are:

- Patent law
- Trade Secret Law
- Federal Patent or Data Policies
- Copyright Law

On the other hand, the legal disciplines ordinarily identified with a later, exploitive phase are:

- Antitrust Law
- Taxation
- Trademark and Unfair Competition Law
- Federal Regulatory Law

We must keep in mind, however, that the legal disciplines that are characteristically identified with different phases of the innovation cycle tend to overlap and interact. Consequently, the findings of this study will concern intersecting issues. A graphic representation (Figure 1-1) expresses the scope of the study. Utilization of a technological innovation is taken as that phase of product development that begins sometime after an innovation has been reduced to practice and ends when marketable goods or services become commercially available.

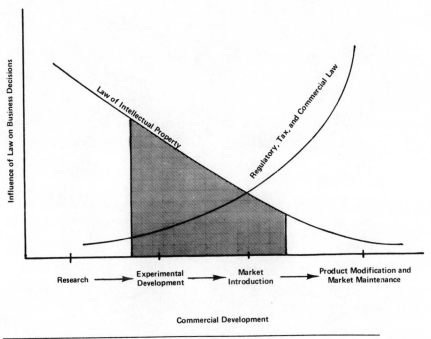

---

[1]Shaded area represents the scope of this study.

Figure 1-1. Utilization and the Law

2 Summary of Findings

Background studies performed under the National Science Foundation's experimental research and development incentive program tend to define issues rather than recommend solutions. Typically, the end product is an experiment, or series of experiments, designed to empirically validate the findings of the study. Three experiments were described in the report upon which this book is based; here, the findings only are presented.

The data of the 1968 government patent policy study showed that patent rights play widely different roles in the business affairs of commercial and educational organizations. We fully expected, and were not disappointed, to have that finding confirmed by this study of legal incentives and barriers. The attitude of an organization toward patent rights is generally typical of its attitude toward the entire law of intellectual property. In both studies the widest divergence of opinion was found between educational and nonprofit institutions, which can achieve utilization of their inventions only by licensing others, and industrial firms, which are able to promote utilization through direct use and licensing. The broad statistical base of the patent policy study provided a perspective from which to evaluate the findings of the present study. Without this base, the findings of the legal incentives study would have to be regarded as anecdotal and peculiar to the scattered sectors of the economy from which they were drawn. Given the earlier work as a pedestal, however, we are able to survey the industrial consequences of the law over a somewhat broader landscape.

Briefly, the study findings are as follows:

- *Innovations that are adequately financed and intelligently marketed are able to circumvent any inconveniences created by intellectual property law.*

Industrial firms place differing weights on the extent to which the inability to secure exclusive proprietary rights acts as a barrier to commercial utilization. This weight is influenced, but not controlled, by whether they are heavily engaged in government contracting.[1] At one extreme are firms that rely heavily on intellectual property rights and would hesitate to invest in an invention in which they could not obtain exclusive rights. At the other are firms whose markets are so secure that they attach little or no importance to legal protection of innovation and, in some instances, innovation itself. In between are firms for whom the law of intellectual property provides a variety of incentives, very few of which are concerned with commercial utilization. Regardless of the attitude

7

of the firm toward legal protection, however, it appears that innovations that are adequately financed and intelligently marketed invariably circumvent any inconveniences created by intellectual property law. Generally speaking, the views of various firms considered in this study fall into one of five categories.

1. *Adherence to the legal forms of protection of intellectual property does not necessarily imply any interest in substantive protection of innovation.* —One group of firms showed a relative lack of interest in legal protection simply because they are not innovative (electric utilities, for example) or because the protection available is so inadequate that they have learned to survive without it (data processing companies, for example). Among data processing firms, it was found that the mode selected for protecting computer software is as likely to be governed by a desired characterization of their product for tax purposes as for safeguarding or transferring technology.

2. *Companies in established industries with a low level of innovation are more interested in establishing a market lead than in securing exclusive rights. There is no evidence that antitrust actions brought against such firms induce utilization of technology.* —In a second group of firms high technology is secondary to broad technical and management competence in maintaining their position in commercial markets. This is true in the coal and steel industries and, to a degree, in the automotive industry. For large companies in established industries with a low level of innovation, the typical legal categorization of intellectual property is neither patent nor trade secret but industrial know-how. Inventions are not as important to these companies in sustaining sales or selling new products as is basic engineering management and production capability. Innovations are incorporated into product modifications or in new models with little consideration for legal protection. Getting a new idea into the marketplace first is regarded as more important than assuring that the company has exclusive rights to it. Antitrust actions brought against such firms may control monopoly and promote competition, but the utilization of technology opened by the consent decrees is negligible.

3. *Proprietary rights are far less important than marketing considerations and investment requirements.* —This third group of firms considers proprietary rights as trading material for cross-licenses with competitive firms. Ownership of rights is a relatively minor factor for new-product utilization compared with the market considerations and investment requirements associated with the commercialization of the innovation. This was true of the automotive industry and characterized the behavior of the aerospace contractors in one of the antitrust cases. At least with such firms, and perhaps for a larger group as well, antitrust actions that are intended to promote competition in research by preventing research pools simply do not have the same consequences as actions that prevent collusion in the marketing of developed products.

4. *The utilization of innovations is not necessarily influenced by the availability of legal protection to established firms.* —This group of firms actively

seeks legal protection to establish and maintain a proprietary position in new technologies, as well as in established market areas. Invariably, however, estimates of market potential and corporate investment requirements are the major determinants of which products are developed. In the petroleum industry, for example, the influence of the law is of a very low order. Given a situation in which all other economic and technical factors are considered equal, an overwhelming majority of companies agreed that the availability of protection for intellectual property does not appreciably influence the utilization of innovations.

5. *The availability of legal protection may be critical to smaller firms and to larger firms entering marginal markets. In some instances, antitrust actions may have a negative effect on utilization.* —This last group of firms regards some form of protection as essential to their business activities. Just how essential this is tends to be a function of the extent to which new capital investment to finance innovation is a market requirement. Although it is not strictly related to the size of the firm, a greater sensitivity to the requirement for capital was found in the smaller firms in the study. In our sample the medical instrumentation market was supplied by relatively small scientific instrument manufacturers. It is arguable with regard to this industry that even when antitrust actions increase competition and reduce monopoly, they may actually have a negative effect on the utilization of innovations. (It may be somewhat disconcerting for some to discover that laws and rulings designed principally to break the monopoly power of large companies often have a deleterious effect on commercial utilization by small companies.) Trade secrets as well as patents are highly regarded by the scientific instrument firms. However, it does not follow that the invalidation of patents will promote the use of trade secrets or that reducing the scope of state trade secret laws will increase the number of patent applications. The decision to file a patent application or treat an invention as a trade secret is more closely related to the technology involved, and to institutional and industrial traditions, than to the state of the law.

Utilization of technology means only that an innovative product or process has moved from the laboratory to the marketplace. It does not imply that a quality product is available to the buying public at a reasonable price. We found that the interests of competition, control of monopoly, and technology utilization do not always march in step. There must often be tradeoffs between competition and monopoly control, on the one hand, and utilization on the other. Unfortunately, policy decisions must frequently be made as to whether the advantages of utilization offset the risks of concentrating economic power, or conversely, whether the advantages of competition make it worthwhile to discourage utilization.

- *The utilization of innovations may remotely depend upon an unspoken faith in the purposes of the law, but this faith bears little relation to the substance of the law.*

Most of the firms interviewed expressed strong opinions regarding recent developments in the law of intellectual property, but then again, "firms" do not give interviews. People do. The executives and lawyers who discuss these topics are usually those who understand them, but their expressions of concern did not necessarily imply that their firms' industrial behavior would be equal to the measure of expressed concern. On the contrary, it would appear that although changes in the laws of intellectual property profoundly affect the rights of parties to disputes, they have little direct influence on the rate of utilization of innovations. For example, if state trade secret laws were invalidated by federal patent law, leaving an individual free to steal technology his former employer considered proprietary, it would be expected that a few Samuel Slaters might set up a few new textile mills[2]—a good thing for competition, but of small consequence to utilization. Similarly, if the life of a patent (currently 17 years) were reduced to 13 years from the grant or extended to 20 years from the filing date, the period of prosecution would be affected, but the influence on utilization would still be negligible. Changes in legal detail appear to affect utilization only in marginal cases and special sectors of the economy, such as universities and nonprofit research institutions.

- *In general, the laws of intellectual property significantly affect the personal rights of parties to such property and the commerical rights of firms to innovations that have already reached the stage of commercial utilization.*

The industrial world is primarily interested in technological content and is highly sensitive to technology utilization and transfer, irrespective of legal format or detail. Government policies that encourage utilization are those which actively promote technology. The curtailment or denial of exclusive rights to an innovation plays a marginal role at best, and only under certain market conditions. Reformers would do well to observe that these conditions more often prevail for small companies than for large ones. The law has a negligible effect either as an incentive or a barrier to the progress of an innovation from its reduction to practice until its commercial introduction.

3 Legal Parameters

This chapter describes the legal parameters within which intellectual property is protected and utilized. The manner in which the law may be considered as either an incentive or a barrier to the utilization of technological innovation is discussed, and the various legal options for protection are introduced.

Incentives

In general, the law mandates some kinds of behavior and prohibits other kinds. Decision making in a free society takes place between the extremes of the obligatory and the forbidden. If legal incentives are considered in the familiar context of economic and personal incentives—as attractive inducements to a desired determination—then the "incentive" of the law may be too subtle to measure.[1]

Generally speaking, one of the functions of a fair and equitable legal system is to help create and preserve a social system in which people will take economic risks which might otherwise not be undertaken. There are relatively few instances in which the law operates as a positive incentive. Taxation, which provides definite incentives to where and how capital shall be invested, is one notable exception to the general rule. Regulatory and antitrust laws, which by prohibiting certain behavior narrow the field of alternative behavior, are more questionable exceptions.

The law of intellectual property, per se, does not serve as an inducement either to create or to exploit. It is not believed that any technician ever pursued a line of inquiry *because* patent or trade secret protection was available. It is not believed that any business ever marketed a process or a product *because* it could legally protect them. The incentives to utilize technology are profit and recognition, to which intellectual property rights have only an indirect and tenuous relationship. Nevertheless, some would attribute greater powers of inducement to the laws of intellectual property than are found to operate in actual practice. For example, it is often argued that if all issued patents were rigidly valid, R&D budgets might be increased. Similarly, some maintain that the limitation of antitrust laws to patent-licensing arrangements is required to provide greater financial incentives to innovation. Conversely, others argue that relaxation of antitrust laws is less likely to increase utilization than to encourage the use of patents to create monopoly and decrease competition.

11

All of these traditionally held beliefs are questionable, as revealed in the study. The availability of legal protection is not the mother of invention. On the other hand, the inability to secure legal protection may discourage the pursuit of a line of inquiry or cause the abandonment of potential utilization—but then the law is serving as a barrier, rather than as an incentive. That, at least, was taken as axiomatic in the present study, which accentuates the negative side of the equation because legal barriers are more directly amenable to study than legal incentives.

Barriers

It is not difficult to discover legal barriers in the law of intellectual property. When a patent or a copyright grants a monopoly to an inventor or to an author, it creates a barrier to the potential infringer. The infringer may feel that the legal monopoly inhibits utilization. The theory of the system, however, is that granting a proprietary right to some and denying it to others encourages utilization. When a court enjoins a former employee from divulging trade secrets to his new employer, from the defendant's point of view utilization is frustrated. From the plaintiff's it is encouraged.

Some have argued that the system itself frustrates utilization. The President's Commission on the Patent System faced that issue squarely in 1966 and determined that the patent system, albeit imperfect and subject to abuse, "is capable of continuing to provide an incentive to research, development, and innovation."[2] Only recently the Supreme Court has been obliged to consider the compatibility of trade secret law and patent law in *Kewanee Oil v. Bicron.*[3] Suffice it to say, this study is not concerned with those barriers created by the law which conform to the spirit of legal protection of intellectual property. Rather, it is concerned with the less-than-wondrous ways in which the law bars, or is alleged to bar, the utilization of technology when in theory it should not do so.

Options for Protection of
Intellectual Property

For purposes of delineation and exposition, this study has been organized according to the major subjects of the law of intellectual property, all of which are inextricably interrelated. The term "innovation" has been taken to mean simply an advance in the state of the art, without regard to patentability. (The term "invention" refers only to those innovations that are patentable.) Figure 3-1 is a graphic representation of the relationships among the various options for protection of intellectual property discussed below.

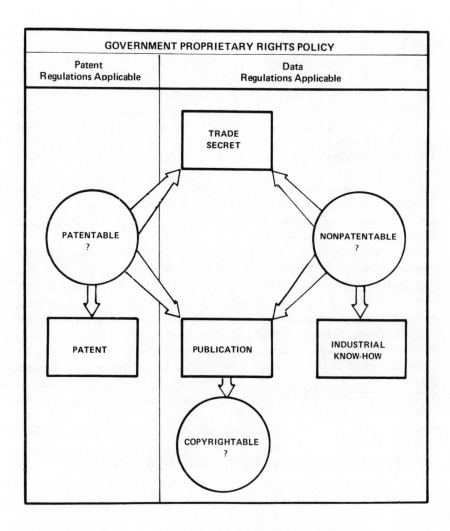

Figure 3-1. Legal Alternatives for Protection of Intellectual Property

If an innovation is patentable, the inventor has at least three options:

1. He may file a patent application within one year of first public use or disclosure.
2. He may forgo the patent monopoly and elect to publish his invention. (A small category of inventions may be protected by copyright or design patent.)
3. He may keep his invention a trade secret.

It is customary practice in some industries—chemical processing, for example—to elect to protect patentable inventions as secrets because it is difficult or impossible to detect infringement of patented property.

In ordinary commercial practice, if an innovation is not patentable, the innovator still has two of the three options available in the case of the patentable invention; that is, trade secret and publication. In at least one instance—computer programs (which are discussed at some length in Chapter 8)—the copyrighted publication is a major form of protection. Generally speaking, however, copyright law is involved with the *expression* of ideas rather than the content of the ideas expressed. In some instances the nonpatentable innovation, although lacking the technical dignity of a trade secret, not to mention the aura of an invention, may nevertheless have considerable commercial importance as "know-how." "Industrial know-how" is a combination of technical and managerial processes, and is often regarded as proprietary in the work of commerce.[4]

All of the legal options, with the exception of patent, are encompassed in the regulatory concept of "technical data" that is used by some of the government agencies that sponsor research. The Department of Defense, for example, defines data as recorded information used to define a design and to produce, support, maintain, or operate equipment. It includes all modes of representation, whether textual, graphic, machine recorded, or even retained in a computer memory. Whether the technical information is otherwise protected or protectable by copyright, trade secret, or as industrial know-how is irrelevant to the data concept.[5]

The options expressed in Figure 3-1 relate commercial and government terminology in the context of the lawyer's question: "How can this innovation be protected?" If the innovation is patentable, shall a patent application be filed, shall the invention be published, or shall it be protected as a trade secret? If published, is it dedicated to the public or can it be protected by copyright?

4 Research Methodology

The folklore of intellectual property invariably includes tales of inventions that are suppressed by companies out of fear that an improvement will adversely affect sales of a marketed product or process. There are also stories of trade secrets so well kept that they never slip into the public domain and of masterpieces destroyed before they are published.[1] We are satisfied that there is more than a germ of truth behind the folklore; however, in a preliminary phase of this study hard evidence of permanent suppression of high technology was extraordinarily difficult to find.

Of far greater significance is the use of legal power to block the commercial utilization of *disclosed* technology that threatens the market structure of established industry. The removal of such blocks encourages the utilization of supporting technology and sometimes leads to the establishment of entirely new industries. Three modern classics from the background literature, discussed in Chapter 5, are the telephone interconnect industry, the community antenna television industry (CATV), and the computer software industry. However, the issues of fact and law regarding intellectual property raised by these cases are, for the most part, problematical in nature. The birth of these new industries from the removal of legal blocks represents a relatively unique development in the laws of intellectual property.

The main thrust of this study is concerned with more prevalent questions associated with intellectual property rights and utilization of technology. The following sections describe the data collection methods in the three areas of intellectual property law into which the study has been organized. It should be emphasized that these categories were chosen for purposes of presentation of study findings. The categories are not neatly bounded, for the laws of intellectual property are intricately interconnected and overlapping.

Patent Policy

The discussion of patent policy, Chapter 6, is addressed to two distinct areas: (1) the patent/antitrust interface and (2) government policy and patent licensing. A major proportion of the effort in this segment of the study is devoted to the first area, in which the point of departure was selected antitrust cases in high technology related to national goals:

Lead Case	Specific Technology	National Goal
U.S. v. College of American Pathologists (The "Pathologists Case")	Medical Instrumentation	Public Health
U.S. v. Automobile Manufacturers Association, et al. (The "Smog Case")	Automotive Emission	Environmental Protection
U.S. v. United Aircraft Corporation (The "Fuel Cell Case")	Fuel Cells	Energy Conservation

In addition to general research and interviews, the methodology for the patent policy part of the study consisted of:

- Study of the pleadings and decisions in each of the above cases.
- Interviews with representatives of the industries involved to gauge the significance of the consent decrees.
- Validation of interview results by comparison with data from other phases of this study with the findings of other studies.
- Monitoring of licensing and developmental activity before and after the court cases.

Beside the three lead cases, which were uncovered through interviews with the Antitrust Division of the Department of Justice, an effort was made to discover relevant pending cases in the federal courts. Searches of federal court dockets were conducted in the District Courts of Boston, St. Louis, Chicago, the District of Columbia, and San Francisco. These searches were performed to uncover information about litigation involving patent cases (and other intellectual property cases under federal jurisdiction) which allege or imply that the operation of the law creates a barrier to the utilization of technology. The effort was abandoned for three reasons:

- The inconsistent manner in which federal court records are maintained in various districts required extremely time-consuming searches by staff attorneys.
- The information revealed in court pleadings was rarely so complete as to set forth any allegation implying frustrated utilization.
- Field data from other aspects of the study began to support a preliminary thesis which strongly suggested the improbability of finding such cases at all.

Negative propositions are not provable by a mere absence of data. However, even if one does not accept the questionable proposition that the failure to find a tree proves that no tree exists, it is certainly arguable that the failure to find a tree proves the nonexistence of a forest. Thus the research for the patent/antitrust interface area was confined primarily to the three lead cases.

At the same time that data coming from the patent/antitrust section of the study (and from the trade secret part below) seemed to indicate that the impact of the law of intellectual property on business decisions affecting technology utilization was trivial, data coming from the patent licensing section of the study pointed in the opposite direction. The methodology of this section consisted of:

- Review of the licensing policies and practices of eleven government agencies.
- Attendance at the NASA Patent Licensing Conference (New England region) and the annual meeting of the American Patent Law Association.
- Discussion of licensing developments with members of the patent bar and officers of the Licensing Executives Society.
- Review of university patent licensing practices.
- Interviews with industry representatives to gauge the significance of recent cases. (This research overlapped the patent/antitrust section.)

Trade Secrets and Industrial Know-How

Trade secret case data, which are set forth in Chapter 7, were investigated in six major industrial states: California, Illinois, Massachusetts, New York, Pennsylvania, and Texas. For the reasons noted above relating to the abandonment of federal court docket searches, state court docket searches proved equally nonproductive. A pilot effort in the Massachusetts Superior Court (the major trial court of general jurisdiction over trade secret cases in Massachusetts) convinced the project staff that the pleadings of unreported cases did not reveal sufficient substantive information for the purposes of the study. Since attorneys representing the litigants declined to discuss pending cases, the methodology was modified to use reported cases and to gain direct access to industry.

Although the subject matter of most trade secret cases arises under state law, many of the cases tend to find their way into federal court on the grounds of "diversity jurisdiction"—where the litigants are domiciled in different states. Many of the more important cases are therefore reported in the United States Patent Quarterly (U.S.P.Q.), which regularly reports all patent and copyright cases. All current cases in the First, Second, Third, Sixth, Seventh, and Ninth Federal Circuits in the following fields were searched.

U.S.P.Q.	
68.901	Unfair Competition, Trade Secrets, General
68.903	Confidential Disclosure
68.905	Disclosure by Employees
68.909	Discovery by Fair and Unfair Means
68.911	Freed by Patent or Disclosure
68.913	Parties Bound

Five cases of possible interest arose during 1973, in addition to the case of *Kewanee Oil Co. v. Bicron* then pending before the U.S. Supreme Court. (Two of the five involved allegations of misuse of proprietary data by a government agency.) Beside the cases reported in U.S.P.Q., the staff analyzed in detail the trade secret elements of the 217-page decision in the private antitrust action of the *Telex Corporation v. IBM* handed down by the Oklahoma District Court in September 1973.

In addition to the case searches, a survey was conducted in collaboration with the Patent, Trademark & Copyright Research Institute (PTC) of the Franklin Pierce Law Center (formerly of George Washington University). The PTC intellectual property questionnaire, and a companion interview program by Harbridge House, were designed to determine the extent to which major industries relied on trade secret protection as preferable to patent protection (or vice versa).

Another principal data source for the trade secret phase of the study was a special inquiry into the treatment of trade secrets at the Federal Trade Commission (FTC). This consisted of interviews with a number of FTC attorneys who deal with matters of trade secrets in order to uncover issues related to the law, FTC policies and practice, and FTC opinions on trade secrets. In addition, the most recent cases were reviewed and literature on the FTC and trade secrets was surveyed. The issue of confidential treatment of trade secrets has arisen more frequently in proceedings before the FTC than in proceedings before any other governmental agency. Consequently, while the practices and rules that have developed in FTC proceedings are not necessarily a model, they do serve as a repository of case law and administration, and form the basis for applications for protection in other agencies.

Copyright and Data

The scope of this study is limited to the utilization of technological innovation; thus it is much narrower than the full range of protection of copyright law,[2] but substantially broader than the technology encompassed by patent law. Copyright law is concerned with the mode of expression (including technological modes); patent law is concerned with the content of an innovation. In one unique instance of high technology, form and content are merged: that is, computer programming.

For the most part, the methodology used to uncover information on copyright and data consisted of a survey of the membership of the National Association of Data Processing Service Organizations (ADAPSO) to determine current industrial attitudes and behavior related to the protection of software.

The copyright and data part of the study also discusses active and passive data policies of the federal government, with particular reference to the National

Aeronautics and Space Administration (NASA) and the National Technical Information Service (NTIS) of the Department of Commerce. NASA's data policies were studied by means of a literature search and also through the attendance of members of the project staff at several NASA Regional Technology Utilization Conferences. NTIS data policies were uncovered through literature search and personal interviews with NTIS personnel.

5 Breaking the Barriers

Three events that occurred in the late sixties are illustrative of the way in which the law presumably acted to knock down barriers to innovation. That is, they involved situations where technology was developed but not (in terms of ultimate potential) widely utilized, and where a legal decision created a more favorable environment for diffusion. In two of the events, the decisions were judicial: *Fortnightly Corp. v. United Artists Television,*[1] a Supreme Court case, and the *Carterfone* case,[2] decided by the Federal Communications Commission. The third event, the IBM "unbundling" of computer services, was a management decision made under certain legal pressures.

In the *Fortnightly* case, decided in 1968, the Supreme Court had to consider, in the words of Justice Fortas, "how a technical, complex, and specific Act of Congress, The Copyright Act, which was enacted in 1909, applies to one of the recent products of scientific and promotional genius, CATV."[3] Fortnightly the owner and operator of community antenna television (CATV) systems, was sued by United Artists for copyright infringement. The activities took place in Clarksburg and Fairmont, West Virginia, where because of the hilly terrain, residents could not receive broadcasts from outside the immediate area with ordinary rooftop antennas. Fortnightly erected antenna systems on the hills above both cities to provide its customers, through a cable service, with broadcasts from several larger cities. The broadcasts included motion pictures on which United Artists held the copyright. The originating stations were licensed by United to broadcast these movies; however, the licenses did not authorize, and in some cases specifically prohibited, carriage by CATV systems. At no time did Fortnightly obtain a license.

The trial court ruled in favor of United on the issue of copyright infringement, and was upheld in the Court of Appeals. The case reached the Supreme Court, and in the words of Justice Fortas, the parties

. . . on the one hand . . . darkly predicted that the imposition of full liability upon all CATV operations could result in the demise of this new, important instrument of mass communications; or in its becoming a tool of the powerful networks which hold a substantial number of copyrights on materials used in the television industry. On the other hand, it is foreseen that a decision . . . [favorable to CATV] would permit such systems to overpower local broadcasting stations which must pay, directly or indirectly, for copyright licenses and with which CATV is in increasing competition.[4]

The Solicitor General filed an amicus brief requesting a compromise solution, which, in effect, asked the court to "stay its hand because . . . the matter is not susceptible of definitive resolution in judicial proceedings and plenary consideration . . . [might] prejudice the ultimate legislative solution."[5] None of the justices agreed, however.[6] Fortas, a minority of one, took the position that pending a legislative resolution of the complex, competing considerations of copyright, communications, and antitrust policy, the court should follow earlier precedents and hold that CATV used mechanical equipment to extend a broadcast to a significantly wider audience, and that this constituted "performance" of a copyrighted work within the meaning of the statute. The majority, however, in a five-to-one decision, reversed the lower courts, noting that broadcasters have been judicially treated as exhibitors (who "perform") and viewers as members of the theater audiences (who "do not perform"). CATV, it concluded, essentially did no more than enhance the viewers' capacity to receive; it did not broadcast or rebroadcast, but simply carried without editing whatever was received. Hence it fell on the viewers' side of the line and, accordingly, infringed no copyright. Largely as a result of this decision, CATV was launched as a viable industry.

The *Carterfone* case began as an antitrust action by Carterfone against American Telephone and Telegraph Company. The district court, while reserving antitrust jurisdiction, referred the matter to the Federal Communications Commission (as the agency of primary jurisdiction) for prior resolution of important issues in the field of telephone communications.

The "Carterfone" is a device designed to connect a regular telephone subscriber to a two-way radio at a base station serving a mobile radio system. The telephone user calls the base station, where an operator inserts the handset of his telephone into the Carterfone device. This device controls a two-way radio set which transmits when the telephone party is speaking and receives when the radio party is speaking. The base station operator can monitor the conversation and disconnect when the communication is finished.

The dispute centered around the legality of a part of the telephone company's tariff which provided that "no equipment, apparatus, circuit, or device not furnished by the telephone company shall be attached to or connected with the facilities furnished by the telephone company, whether physically, by induction, or otherwise . . . "[7] The Commission found that Carterfone filled a need and that it did not adversely affect the telephone system. The tariff cited above, in prohibiting the use of Carterfone devices, was determined to be unreasonably and unduly discriminatory in its application to Carterfone. (Since the tariff had originally been submitted by AT&T and not imposed by the Commission, the Commission declared it should be stricken and left the burden on AT&T to submit a revised one.) In short, AT&T policy constituted unreasonable interference with a subscriber's right to use telephone service in a way that was privately beneficial without being publicly detrimental.

AT&T argued (1) that it had to have complete control for maintenance purposes and (2) that development of telephone systems would be retarded, since independent equipment suppliers would tend to resist changes that would make equipment obsolete. The Commission was unimpressed with these arguments. On the first point, it stated that the telephone company could prevent practices that actually caused harm (there was no evidence of that in the Carterfone case) and set up reasonable standards. On the second point (which appeared to be speculation, with no evidence offered), the Commission stated that if independent suppliers offered products that might be made obsolete by AT&T system changes, this was simply a business risk.

AT&T's application for rehearing (based on independents "skimming the cream" and conceivable adverse economic effects on AT&T) was denied.[8] The effect of the decision was the creation of the telephone interconnect industry.

International Business Machines Corporation announced in June 1969 that it would separately price most new computer programs and various systems engineering and educational services. Previously, these services had been available to IBM customers (purchasers and lessors of its hardware) without separate charge. At the same time, IBM reduced sales and rental prices for its machines. This policy change, involving separate pricing of computer hardware and related software, was called "unbundling."

Even though the computer software industry (that is, the complex of firms concerned with the technology of using computers) was thriving before 1969, the IBM decision was nevertheless similar in effect to the decisions in the *Fortnightly* and *Carterfone* cases; it paved the way for wider use of a developed technology. With services and hardware separately priced, there was greater incentive for independent firms to compete with IBM and other manufacturers in developing computer programs and in the overall design of information and data processing systems. It is possible that purely business considerations could have justified the IBM decision (under the theory that the services end of the business, by standing on its own feet, would become more efficient, more responsive to user needs, and hence more profitable). However, the fact that it was made when several lawsuits against IBM, alleging antitrust violations, were pending or imminent, suggests that legal factors may also have had some influence on corporate policy.

These cases are generally credited with opening up the CATV, interconnect, and computer software industries. In all three cases, the technology had been developed and had enjoyed some utilization prior to the legal or (in the case of unbundling) managerial breakthrough. Although *Fortnightly* involved copyright law, all the cases veer toward the right side of the shaded area of principal interest discussed in Chapter 1.[9] They are displayed in their own context in Figure 5-1.[10] As such they should be regarded as important background to collected data.

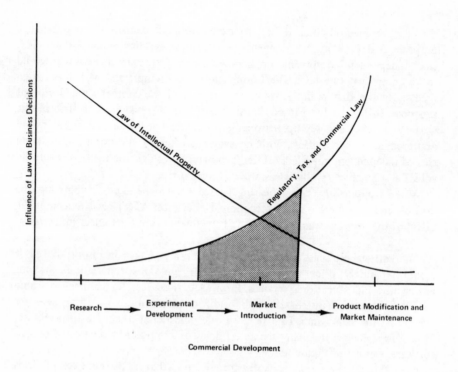

Figure 5-1. Breaking the Barriers to Utilization

Part II
The Data

... The Judge left the Court, looking deeply disgusted:
But the Snark, though a little aghast,
As the lawyer to whom the defense was entrusted,
Went bellowing on to the last.

—Lewis Carroll, "The Hunting of the Snark"

6 Patents

Patents and Antitrust Laws

A defendant's classical defenses to a patent infringement action are (1) to deny that his product or process infringes the plaintiff's patent; (2) to challenge the validity of the patent alleged to be infringed; and (3) to assert that the plaintiff is in violation of the antitrust laws. The antitrust defense usually consists of claims that the plaintiff is attempting to extend the scope of his monopoly beyond the monopoly legally authorized by the patent. The issue of conflict between antitrust laws and patent laws arises out of the fundamental fact that the purpose of antitrust laws is to prevent unreasonable restraint of trade. The purpose of patent laws, on the other hand, is to encourage inventions by providing a monopoly which inherently does restrain trade.[1]

The reconciliation of differences is made more difficult by the fact that patent laws create property rights and antitrust laws regulate commercial behavior. The conflict was not foreseen when the Sherman Act of 1890 was passed 100 years after the first patent act, and the two fields of law peacefully coexisted for half a century. Increasingly, however, the Antitrust Division of the Department of Justice has felt that patent monopoly is being unreasonably extended by large corporations in restraint of trade, and consequently the patent bar has become concerned about the whittling away of the power of the patent. At the same time, the federal courts have invalidated 79 percent of all patents whose validity has been challenged on appeal. Small wonder, then, that patents have become mere "trading material" in antitrust actions in which a defendant agrees to dedicate a portion of its patent portfolio to the public if the government will agree to dismiss or modify its suit.

An antitrust action is concerned principally with monopoly and competition and only peripherally with the utilization of innovations. A defendant may have suppressed his technology as a device to secure monopoly power, but there is no law that requires the "working" of either patents or trade secrets in the United States. Even if a defendant has fully utilized his technology, he may still have improperly restrained others from entering the market. The issue of utilization may also fall somewhere in between these two extremes; that is, the speed of utilization may have been retarded by the defendant's monopoly position. In a fully exploited market, merely ordering a defendant to open his patents is not likely to reduce monopoly or increase competition. Consent decrees that include patent dedication are meaningful only if they increase utilization.

27

In order to determine the effect of antitrust consent decrees on the utilization of technology, the project staff held a series of conferences with the Antitrust Division. Three cases were selected for discussion: the first involved patents and trade secrets; the second was purely regulatory; and the third involved patents and know-how. The settlement of these cases ought to have resulted in the removal of barriers to utilization. However, as will be seen in the following sections, this did not happen.

The Fuel Cell Case

A fuel cell is a device for the production of electricity through a chemical reaction of fuels supplied from outside of the cell. Unlike a battery, which is exhausted when chemical energy is converted to electrical energy, a fuel cell will provide electricity as long as fuel is supplied to it. Around 1959, the United Aircraft Corporation acquired exclusive patent rights to an invention known as the "Bacon" fuel cell.

In 1961 both United and TRW, Inc., submitted proposals to NASA under the Apollo program. TRW, like United, proposed to use a fuel cell of the Bacon type. United and TRW were the only two bidders who submitted competitive proposals employing this technical approach. Each company was in constant communication with the other regarding their fuel cell "competition" during negotiation of the government contract. Eventually TRW dropped out of the negotiations. The award was made to United on the basis of its previous experience in the field and the fact that it had invested over one million dollars of its own money in research. Twelve years later, in April 1973, the Antitrust Division filed an action against United to compel a public dedication of fuel cell technology.

The basis of the action was an allegation by the Department of Justice that United had effectively suppressed all fuel cell competition through collusion with TRW. The two companies were alleged to have agreed that all research and development work would be turned over to United and all data would become the exclusive property of United. An industry spokesman claimed, however, that the real basis for the action actually arose out of an investigation of the Aircraft Industry Association for alleged antitrust activities. Although that investigation wound up nowhere, the industry contends that the Department of Justice had to make some party account for all the time and energy that had been invested in the matter. Suffice it to say, a consent judgment was entered 60 days after filing of the suit, ordering United to reveal its fuel cell technology. The Department of Justice regards the judgment as opening to the public a technology that may suggest new energy sources by 1980. The defendant believes that the consent decree was of little benefit to anyone and is not likely to affect the future development of fuel cell technology.

The decree itself enjoined the defendant from entering into confidential agreements concerning fuel cell technology, from using or threatening to use its economic power to prevent others from engaging in fuel cell research, and from acquiring a significant interest in any other company involved in fuel cell technology. In addition, United is required to grant a nonexclusive royalty-free license to any applicant for any patented technology arising out of the Apollo contracts. Most significantly, United's technical data on fuel cells are to be licensed to any applicant who is willing to pay a one-time royalty fee of $25,000.

The original patent, of course, had only a few years to run at the time the Justice Department brought its action in 1973. It is of no small significance that by then at least 90 percent of the fuel cell technology was regarded by the defendant as involving industrial know-how rather than any high level of innovation. United's assessment was corroborated by one of the leading academic authorities on fuel cells, who revealed to the project staff that the technology had far outstripped the underlying scientific systems. He further stated that the failure of private industry, or the government, to invest in further basic research had resulted in an enormous investment in public and private funds with very little possibility of return. It is certainly true that, at least since the issuance of the consent decree in June 1973, there has been no great rush to secure royalty-free licenses from United, nor has anyone offered to pay the first $25,000 for a peek at the data. At this time there are only three companies known to be involved in any aspect of fuel cell technology: United, Exxon, and Westinghouse. (The latter appears concerned only with high-temperature fuel cells.)

There has never been any kind of promotion or policing of the decree by either the defendant or the Department of Justice. While it is still too early to pass final judgment on whether the opening of the patent and data portfolio has advanced the utilization of technology, thus far even the "one small step" is yet to be taken.

The Pathologists Case

The American College of Pathologists is a professional society of doctors of pathology. It determines educational standards and influences the conduct and ethics of that branch of medicine, including the condition of operation of hospital laboratories, which are a principal market for medical instrumentation. The equipment in such laboratories, ranging from relatively simple centrifuges and autoclaves to extremely sophisticated spectrochemical and photometric devices, is manufactured by an energetic and innovative industry.[2]

One of the rules of the College was that all medical laboratories had to operate under the supervision of a fully accredited pathologist. Since there are many more laboratories than pathologists, it often happened that a doctor other than a pathologist, or even a senior medical technician, really supervised the laboratory. However, the exercise of "responsibility" on the part of the pathologists was an extremely profitable paper operation, and it allegedly restrained other qualified persons from opening new laboratories.

Under pressure of litigation by the Antitrust Division, the College finally dropped its requirement that medical laboratories be directed only by a physician who was a fellow of the College. Although the case did not directly involve the dedication of a patent portfolio, it might be expected that the destruction of a monopoly—and the restoration of a free market in which patents are aggressively pursued by the industrial supliers—would invite increased use of medical instrumentation. However, the interviews with hospital and industrial personnel suggest that the decision had little or no influence on the medical instrumentation market.

To some extent, the medical instrumentation business has grown in spite of the consent decree rather than because of it. This has come about because analytical laboratories often employ innovative technologists, and thus there has always been a substantial amount of in-house development of instrumentation. If the consent decree had any influence on utilization of technological innovations (as measured by inquiries about new products as opposed to orders for known products) it appears to have been negative. When each pathologist was directing several hospital laboratories he looked into every new analytical device that could be used to increase the laboratory output without increasing personnel. This interest seems less pronounced under local hospital administration of the labs. Even assuming that the pathologists case increased competition and reduced monopoly, it had little effect on utilization; what effect it did have was probably negative.

The medical instrumentation market is especially attractive to small companies because of the continuation of government funding (which has been drastically reduced in other fields in recent years). Not only have the scientific instrument companies been going into the laboratory business, but also the laboratories have been going into the instrumentation business. The pace of cross-fertilization was not affected by the decision, and the pathologists and their successors both welcomed the exchange.

The medical instrumentation industry enjoys a relative freedom from regulation which is not shared by its pharmacological counterpart in the public health field. Although patents play an unusually vital role in the innovative instrumentation industry, it is fear of government regulation, rather than the law of intellectual property, that is the potential barrier most viewed with alarm by representatives of the industry. In particular, concern was expressed in several interviews that the entry of the Food and Drug Administration into the field might force out small concerns that could not bear the cost of compliance with regulatory standards. Antitrust was only a remote consideration.

Patents are aggressively pursued by the medical instrumentation industry for traditional offensive (licensing) and defensive purposes. Interest in patenting is diminished, however, in those instances in which title passes to the government because the research was sponsored by HEW, or virtually any other U.S. agency. (Under the President's Patent Memorandum of August 23, 1971, all government agencies are obliged to vest principal or exclusive rights to the government on an invention related to public health.) Under such circumstances, the inventor simply publishes a report of his innovation and fails to point out the technical threshold of "non-obviousness" which is the standard of invention. For example, the extremely creative head of one large hospital laboratory declared that without a right to title he was inclined to publish rather than patent. The instrumentation companies would not invest in the unprotected invention, but at least he would receive recognition from the technical journals. However, when pressed to give examples of technology which, because of the government patent policy, were unmarketed, he referred to the general atmosphere rather than to specific cases. Nevertheless, we found sufficiently broad support for this proposition among small manufacturers to justify the conclusion that in marginal cases the law might well make a difference in the instrumentation industry.

The Smog Case

The industrial climate of the Automobile Manufacturers Association case is at the opposite pole from that of the pathologists case. The latter is characterized by small, aggressive companies with a high degree of innovation, which actively pursue patents for offensive as well as defensive purposes. The former is characterized by several industrial giants with an astonishingly low level of innovation, to whom patents are largely trading material within the industry and in antitrust cases.

In the principal case involving the Automobile Manufacturers Association, the Department of Justice brought an action against the Association and its principal members and joined the entire industry as co-conspirators. The four major U.S. automobile manufacturers were named as defendants. The object of the lawsuit was to eliminate the industrial custom of pooling research, at least so far as it pertained to innovations in automotive emissions. The essence of the government's argument was that the major manufacturers had conspired to prevent or retard pollution control through a pooling technique that guaranteed that no manufacturer would proceed more rapidly than the slowest member of the inside group.[3] The defendants answered that they sought to improve the technology by opening the fruits of their research to the industry. The consent judgment filed in this case required each of the defendants to withdraw from the industry cross-licensing pool. At the same time the defendants were ordered to grant nonexclusive royalty-free licenses to any of the patents in the pool and to open to the public over 100 specified technical reports on automotive pollution control.

For a variety of reasons peculiar to its history, capital structure, and manufacturing and marketing methods, the utilization rate of innovation in the automobile industry is extremely low. (The same was found to be true of the steel industry during the course of the trade secret studies, discussed in Chapter 7.) From interviews with industry leaders, it was concluded that patents are integrated into overall market strategies and are not seriously considered either as a source of new technology or as a significant factor in commercialization. Furthermore, it became evident during patent interviews—and was subsequently confirmed in trade secret interviews—that neither patent *nor* trade secret is a particularly important repository of intellectual property in the automotive industry. Characteristically, for large companies in established industries with a low level of innovation, the principal capital in the technical data bank, so to speak, is neither patent nor trade secret but industrial know-how. We were advised on several occasions that there are no real technical breakthroughs in the automobile industry—only lead time differentials. It appeared to be accepted by the major companies that market position is maintained by making as few significant changes as possible, as inexpensively as possible.

Underlying the action of the Department of Justice was the belief that the key issue was simply the speed of utilization of existing technology rather than further innovation. The industry, however, argued that in 1970, when the Congress set the automotive emission standards for 1975 to 1976, there was no known technology by which to eliminate 97 percent of the hydrocarbons, 96 percent of carbon monoxide, and 93 percent of nitrogen oxide. If the technology did exist for mass production—and most authorities believed that it did[4]—the industry certainly worked at least as hard for a relaxation of the standards as it did to effect compliance.[5] It is probable that the industry has dragged its heels. However, the key question concerns the effectiveness of the Justice antidote; how accurate is the implicit assumption that an antitrust action against technology pools is to utilization as an antitrust action against monopolistic market practices is to competition?

The game was not played out before the rules were changed. But as far as it went, a definite pattern was becoming evident. Even though the opening of technical data in some portions of the smog case decision and the prohibition of sharing in other portions of the decision had little effect on technology utilization, the antitrust action appears to have substantially affected the lead-time factor. All of the automotive companies were working against the 1975 emission standards of the Clean Air Act. Two of the major companies elected to meet the standards through the catalytic converter, a solution all agree is technically inelegant and increases operating costs. The third decided to meet the standards through an engine redesign which would result in more efficient combustion. For a time it appeared likely that the first two companies would be able to meet the 1975 standards and the third would not. This created a dilemma of monumental proportions: If the requirements were not relaxed, then one of the big three could be forced out of business for failure to comply with regulatory standards. If the requirements were relaxed for the one company that was unable to meet the standards in time, then the other two companies would have been at a competitive disadvantage because of the higher costs they had incurred in complying with the law.

Thanks to the petroleum "energy crisis," of 1974 the 1975-1976 standards of the Clean Air Act were relaxed by Congress because the catalytic converter increases gasoline consumption. Thus one can only speculate about what might have been. The dilemma was avoided. The air will become increasingly polluted. And it does not appear that in a regulated environment antitrust actions which are intended to promote competition in research by prohibiting pooling are comparable to similar actions which prevent collusion in the marketing of developed products. Nor do they promote utilization in an oligopolistic market.

Government Policy and Patent Licensing

Five and a half years ago, in the Government patent policy study, Harbridge House reported that the commercial utilization of government-sponsored inventions is very low. Of 2,100 inventions examined in that study, only 55 (2.7 percent) played a critical role in the commercial products in which they were used, as compared to estimated utilization rates of 50 percent or more for inventions developed under private research. The federal government addressed this discovery in the President's Memorandum and Statement of Government Patent Policy of August 23, 1971.[6] The principal difference between the 1971 policy and the 1963 policy it succeeded lies in the government's effort to increase the rate of utilization by offering to industry greater license incentives to utilize government-sponsored research. Since the proclamation of the 1971 policy, the government agencies sponsoring research have begun to publish implementing regulations in the Federal Register and elsewhere.[7] For the most part, these regulations are restatements or paraphrases of the President's policy statement. Some executive agencies, notably the General Services Administration, the National Aeronautics and Space Administration, and the National Technical Information Service of the Department of Commerce have instituted active programs. (The programs of the latter two are described in Chapter 8.)

The policy of waiving government rights to title in patents or granting exclusive licenses to a government contractor has been challenged by critics who contend that such policies are merely a giveaway of government property. The position of the critics was recently sustained in *Public Citizen, Inc., v. Sampson.*[8] In this case, the U.S. District Court for the District of Columbia voided the patent licensing regulations issued by GSA on the grounds that they were an unconstitutional disposition of federal property without Congressional authorization and failed to comply with the public notice requirement of the Administrative Procedure Act.

Since the plaintiff in *Public Citizen* was joined by 11 Congressmen, it is evident that the title-versus-license dispute in government contracting, which has been smoldering since the 1968 Government Patent Policy Study, will be rekindled.[9] This is bad news for two segments of the economy which, in the present study, expressed a high sensitivity to patent protection and government policy: (1) scientific instrumentation industry and (2) the colleges and universities.

During the course of the patent antitrust phase above, and again in the trade secret phase below, the study singles out "medical instrumentation" as a representative public health technology. Actually, medical instrumentation is a market rather than an industry. Strictly speaking, the industry, which sells its measuring and testing devices to hospitals, industrial and government laboratories, and institutions of higher education, is the scientific instrumentation industry. It includes several large electronic and optical firms and scores of small research-based companies in Massachusetts, California, and elsewhere.

Unlike the larger firms, which currently appear to be concerned with alleged Antitrust Division hostility to field-of-use licensing,[10] the smaller companies are anxious about the high cost of protection under patents of increasingly doubtful validity and also about the failure of the government to either adequately fund research or grant sufficient rights to industry under government contracts to attract risk capital. The observations of the half dozen or so firms interviewed may be critically regarded as anecdotal rather than statistically significant. However, their views are consistent and their concern is sincere, as exemplified by an exchange of correspondence between the American Association of Small Research Companies and the National Science Foundation in which the former urged the latter to change its patent policy so that profit-making concerns as well as universities might retain title to inventions arising out of government research.[11] Referring to the impossibility of anticipating all possible circumstances, the NSF pleaded for flexibility in dealing with particular cases and reminded the Association that under the Presidential policy—in cases where a principal purpose of the research is to affect public health—the government will normally take title to incident inventions. In the light of the conclusion reached in the pathologists case (above), *Public Citizen* is probably a step backward for utilization in medical instrumentation.

Inventions arising out of university and nonprofit research do not travel the same route to commercial utilization as do inventions arising out of industrial research.[12] While there is a great deal of variation in the policies and practices of educational and nonprofit research institutions, we found more similarities than differences among them when contrasted with industrial commercialization practices. The nonprofit institutions do not make or sell the products and processes embodying their inventions but must license these inventions in order to have them used. Therefore, these institutions have evolved a variety of licensing techniques to transfer technology from nonprofit research programs to the marketplace.

Some colleges and universities have their own licensing programs. These programs call for processing patents through special administrative units that are responsible directly to the administration of the senior policy-making group in the institution. Other colleges and universities administer patents as a part of the routine duties of established offices and faculty committees. An office of research services, which is responsible for administration of sponsored research, provides the necessary administrative support. Here, as in other institutions that lack formal licensing programs, the administrative arm of the school ensures that pertinent institutional regulations are observed, that there is compliance with invention-reporting requirements of government contracts, and that the rights of the parties involved are guarded in the rare case of a decision to patent an invention.

Many educational institutions administer patent programs through independent foundations for various legal, financial, and policy reasons that are only occasionally related to invention utilization. In these instances, the invention is assigned to the foundation either by the institution or by the inventor himself. The reasons for working through such foundations include:

- Insulating patent funds from use by the state government, or even by the university itself, for purposes other than financing scientific research.
- Creating a buffer between the nonprofit institution and industrial licensees in the event of litigation.
- Limiting contractual and tax liabilities.
- Providing a degree of flexibility in relationships between the nonprofits and industry, which is not possible if the nonprofit institution works alone.
- Facilitating a continuing relationship between the inventor and the licensee in order to develop the invention.

In many instances, a patent administration foundation is created to relieve the institutional administrative staff of the complicated and time-consuming technical and commercial problems of patent management.

The principal agent for the transfer of the patentable products of nonprofit research industry, however, is the patent development firm. Two out of every three academic institutions have contracts with patent development firms. Our investigation was therefore confined to these firms (and one large university which prosecutes its own patents) rather than to the colleges themselves.[13] Some patent development firms serve a restricted clientele or a limited technological market. Only three firms offer their services in invention marketing to all educational institutions, foundations, and nonprofit research corporations. The services of patent development firms include:

- Evaluation of disclosures.
- Assistance in preparation of patent applications.
- Promotion of inventions.
- Negotiation of licenses.
- Distribution of royalties.
- Policing the patent.

The patent development firms act both as a clearinghouse for the nonprofits and as a marketplace for industry. Patents are typically assigned to the firms on a royalty-sharing basis. Patent applications are filed on approximately 10 to 15 percent of the disclosures submitted, and, if present circumstances continue, only one quarter of these patents will ever be licensed.

Inventions arising out of nonprofit research have a distinctly different character than the patentable ideas arising from R&D contracts with industry. In nonprofit research, the end product is normally "software," or scientific findings, and patentable ideas take the form of concepts rather than hardware. In industry R&D, on the other hand, the result is usually "hardware"; a product, process, or component—and a working model, at least—will have been developed.

The task of a nonprofit organization is over and its contract has been fulfilled when the organization submits a research report. Funds are rarely available to reduce the discovery to any practical application, and interest and motivation to seek utilization are often absent. The idea of following an invention through development and production to a marketable product is alien to the academic and nonprofit environment. For this reason, the patent licensing profession refers to academic invention as a "bare-bones patent." Industry must take it from there.

In contrast, under comparable government research contracts, the industry contractor normally seeks to promote follow-on work that will ultimately develop his findings into a product. Should contract research result in an invention with commercial possibilities, financing will normally be secured to develop and exploit it.

Nonprofit research inventions usually require a larger investment for commercialization than industry discoveries because nonprofit inventions are frequently at an earlier stage of development. In our investigation, the nonprofit institutions repeatedly emphasized the additional investment industry has made to develop products based on nonprofit discoveries.

Another characteristic of nonprofit inventions is that they often technically stand alone. Their technical isolation is a major obstacle to utilization, since most inventions are not marketable products in themselves. The industrial product is often protected by a cordon of patents, as illustrated by the list of patents on a packet of Polaroid film. A university invention, on the other hand, is a one-shot patent. Even if the patent specification discloses an ingenious invention, the patent claims that define the scope of the monopoly are likely to be narrowly drawn. Whereas industry will add to its patent arsenal as a product is improved, a university patent, if it is to be licensed at all, must be licensed as a significant advance in the state of the art.

Industry can profitably keep an innovation "on the shelf" until the time is right to market it. Furthermore, cross-licensing agreements between firms extend the economic utility of the industrial patent. Nonprofit inventions, on the other hand, remote from the market to begin with, are perishable if unlicensed, since the nonprofit organizations do not have manufacturing operations. All the above characteristics of inventions developed by nonprofit institutions make them high-risk commercialization ventures.

Another major factor affecting invention utilization by academic institutions is the drive to publish research results. This drive produces a dilemma where utilization of inventions is concerned, since patents are the only protection for the inventions of nonprofit institutions. In the nonprofit environment, there is no economically useful equivalent of "proprietary data" or industrial trade secrets. While industry may benefit from these alternatives to patenting, the secrecy involved is counter to the tradition in university and nonprofit research.

This tradition reflects the relative values that academic institutions place on publishing and patenting the results of their work. Publications are central to scholarly pursuit. Invariably, the results of research, except those limited by the terms of a grant or contract, are fully disclosed through articles in scientific and technical journals. Patents, on the other hand, have traditionally been regarded as irrelevant at best and, at worst, as an indication of unworthy commercial motives. Thus, we found that perhaps the single most difficult task of a university patent administrator was the solicitation of invention disclosures. Even if the inventor was willing to cooperate in the utilization process, it was a familiar story that the university patent office only learned of the invention eight months after publication in a scientific or technical journal.

Under the present law, patent applications must be filed within one year of public disclosure of the invention or the patent will be banned. Thus patentable ideas are frequently lost to an institution's portfolio. The universities, however, have never considered the industrial alternative of delaying publication until a patent is filed, resting on the comfort of one year within which to file an application.[14] On the other hand, if government regulations required disclosure to the government prior to the publication of findings, a serious question of academic freedom might arise.

While nonprofit institutions actively disseminate technology through publication, promoting utilization of a specific invention is another matter. Given the academic preference for publication of research results rather than patenting them, a major problem exists in mounting an effective patent promotion program. Except for a few universities and technical schools, there is currently little active promotion of patents by the academic institutions themselves. This task is largely contracted to a few professional firms which specialize in the promotion of university research.

The critical question concerning utilization is whether patents, given their speculate utility, would be promoted more effectively through government ownership. The DOD, which is a license agency, leaves the patent title and commercial utilization to the private sector. On the other hand, NASA, which is a title agency, has adopted an active utilization policy (described in Chapter 8). In most cases, a substantial private investment is required to commercialize patents, and the nonexclusive licenses offered by such agencies as NASA may not compensate for the development risks involved.

Inventions of public service agencies—such as TVA, HEW, and the Departments of Agriculture and the Interior—may differ from the inventions arising out of research sponsored by mission oriented agencies in two important respects: (1) their close alignment with commercial needs and (2) their greater development and promotion by the agency for public use. Appraisal of public service agencies and their promotional programs suggests that TVA and Department of Agriculture inventions have a good chance of utilization if these agencies not only retain title but also invest in product development and promotion. HEW and Department of the Interior inventions, on the other hand, require strong patent incentives for industry because of high product development costs and minimum development and promotion on the part of the agencies.

Allowing academic and nonprofit institutions to keep title, under these circumstances, offers greater flexibility in providing patent protection to interested developers, when protection is necessary to achieve utilization. Title also motivates the inventor himself to assist in developing the invention for commercial use, because of its potential rewards to him.

7

Trade Secret and Industrial Know-How

Current Legal Issues

The Restatement of Torts defines a trade secret as "any information of peculiar value to its owner, not protected by patent and not generally known or accessible to everyone."[1] Trade secrets last only as long as substantial secrecy is preserved. Ideas in general circulation are obviously in the public domain. By the same token, any person who independently learns a secret may lawfully use it or disclose it to another. The same is true of "know-how," a concept related to the application of technology in an industrial situation rather than to creativity. Know-how is a body of knowledge which often includes bits and pieces of information known in the public domain, records of other industrial application, cost data, and so forth. The main elements of a plaintiff's action in a trade secret or know-how case are (1) proof of discovery of a specific trade secret by unfair means; (2) a disclosure of the trade secret to the defendant in trust or confidence; and (3) the violation of the confidence to others to the injury of the plaintiff. Table 7-1 compares the scope of protection and the legal characteristics of patent and trade secret.

Although a cause of action for the wrongful disclosure of trade secrets has existed since the earliest times,[2] it has only become significant in the United States since the beginning of the twentieth century.[3] But since then, hundreds of cases in the state and federal courts have resulted in entire textbooks on the subject.[4]

The classic trade secret case can be illustrated by presenting the trade secret aspects of the recent celebrated antitrust case of *Telex Corporation v. IBM.*[5] The key issues were raised by IBM as part of its counterclaim to the antitrust action brought by Telex. Telex had a policy of generally following IBM's product leadership and subordinating its own efforts in technological innovation. Telex products were designed as the functional equivalent of previously announced IBM products. A typical finding of fact (F153) was " ... Telex was not primarily interested in new product design or in an advance of the state of the art through technology developed independently, but rather in a ... device copied from IBM's design through utilization of IBM information."

What was IBM's posture with regard to technological development and protection of its position? The U.S. district court judge found little or no evidence that IBM adopted specific programs to throttle or impede general systems competition (as distinguished from "plug-compatible-products" compe-

39

Table 7-1
Comparison of the Salient Characteristics and Protection Afforded by Letters Patent and Trade Secret Principles

	Full Disclosure Required	Disclosure of Discoverer	Level of Invention	Cost to Obtain	Date Protection Commences
PATENTS	Yes	Yes	Relatively high	Relatively expensive	Upon grant of letters patent
TRADE SECRETS	No; unprotected disclosure risks loss	No	Indeterminate, but considerably less than for patents	Indeterminate; cost of maintenance of secrecy must be considered	From research and development stage

	Date Protection Ceases	Duration	Loss by Independent Discovery	Rights Against Independent Discoverers
PATENTS	Expiration of patent or declaration of invalidity	If valid, 17 years	None, if patent valid[a]	Full rights
TRADE SECRETS	As of unprotected disclosure or matter becoming generally known	Indeterminate; may be perpetual	Loss if such discovery becomes so widespread as to be "generally known"	None

Availability of Injunctive Relief	Availability of Damages	Recovery of Attorney's Fees	Criminal Law Protection

		Protection Outside the United States
PATENTS	Yes[b]	Only by further registration in foreign jurisdictions within prescribed period
TRADE SECRETS	Yes	Probably, and if so, without formalities

	License or Sales Revenues Eligible for Capital Gains	Basis for Jurisdiction		
PATENTS	Yes[c]	Registration with U.S. Pat Office[g]	In exceptional case[d]	Not available[e]
TRADE SECRETS	Yes	No comparable basis	Yes[f]	Available at state and federal level

Copyright © 1969, by Matthew Bender & Company, Inc., and reprinted with permission from Milgrim, *Trade Secrets*, Section 8.02 [8]. Selected footnotes have been renumbered for clarity.

[a] Approximately 80 percent of all patent actions reaching the appellate court level have been held invalid. Moreover, even if a patent is valid, competitors may successfully design around it or employ it secretly, as in the case of process patents.

[b] 35 U.S.C. §283.

[c] 35 U.S.C. §284.

[d] 35 U.S.C. §285.

[e] 35 U.S.C. §281 (civil action is patentee's remedy for infringement).

[f] Where defendant is a flagrant wrongdoer, attorney's fees are in order.

[g] See *United States v. Farbenfabriken Bayer, A.G.,* ___ F. Supp. ___ (D.D.C. 1968), Antitrust & Trade Reg. Rep. No. 358, A-9 (question certified to D.C. Cir. whether nonresident patent registrant subject to service of United States antitrust process); *United States v. Glaxo Group, Ltd.,* ___ F. Supp. ___ (D.D.C. 1968), Antitrust & Trade Reg. Rep. No. 356, A-8.

tition). IBM's growth and success, the court found (F112), was due in substantial measure to its skill, industry, and foresight. "In the approximately 20 years that the EDP industry has been in existence IBM has introduced more than 600 products. Some of these products include major technological innovations. By virtue of its own research and development, IBM has obtained more than 10,000 patents which are freely licensed." The court also found that it would be competitively unreasonable and inhibiting to technological development to require IBM to describe all product enhancements that are planned or anticipated to be made to a product during its product life.

Telex strategy in availing itself of IBM confidential data appeared to have two phases: first, to hire people who could provide proprietary business or marketing data on IBM—marketing analyses, financial forecasts, product costs, plans for new products, and so forth; and second, to hire engineers from IBM who could provide technical details of proposed IBM products so that they could be copied and marketed in much less time than if Telex waited for public introduction of the new product. Nearly all the people who left IBM to go to Telex had exit interviews during which the proprietary aspects of IBM data were emphasized. Statements were signed acknowledging this fact, and in many cases the IBM employees had also signed a similar agreement when coming to work for IBM.

The court recognized that the line of demarcation between use of trade secret information and legitimate use of skills acquired on the job was often difficult to draw. Nevertheless, it was clear, in the court's view, that Telex intended to benefit not only from skills legitimately acquired, but also from knowledge it knew existed as trade secret.

IBM was awarded damages for loss of rentals and for unjust enrichment caused by misappropriation of trade secrets and for increased security costs occasioned by Telex's activities. Both sides have appealed to the U.S. Court of Appeals. In addition to determimining the complex antitrust elements, which are being appealed by the defendant, IBM, the court will have to rule on the validity of the trade secrets, which is being appealed by the plaintiff, Telex.

Another current classic involving trade secret is the case of *Kewanee Oil v. Bicron*. To understand the issue and the significance of the data in this intellectual property case, we must go back to the decision of the U.S. Supreme Court in *Lear, Inc., v. Adkins.*[6] This was a patent case which held that the licensee of a patent may avoid further royalty payments, regardless of the provisions of any contract, once a third party proves that the patent is invalid. Regarding a pending patent, however, the court reserved decision on whether the states have the power to enforce contracts under which someone claiming to have a new discovery can obtain payment for disclosing it during the pendency of a patent application, even if the application is subsequently abandoned or the innovation held to be unpatentable. More often than not, an invention is licensed during the pendency of the patent application. But because patent applications are not published by the Patent Office, the distinction between licensing an invention for which a patent has been applied and licensing a trade secret is difficult for a businessman to perceive.

Subsequent to *Lear*, a legal crackdown on trade secrets and know-how followed immediately: a New York federal district court simply denied the licensing ability of any unpatented know-how. However, this decision was reversed by the U.S. Court of Appeals for the Second Circuit in *Painton & Co., Ltd., v. Bourns, Inc.*[7] But again, on May 10, 1973, the U.S. Court of Appeals for the Sixth Circuit, taking its cue from the concurring opinion of Justice Black in *Lear*, went the other way in *Kewanee Oil v. Bicron*, and until the conflict between the two circuits was resolved by the U.S. Supreme Court the trade secret was once again in high jeopardy. The facts of the case were as follows:

Kewanee, through one of its divisions, manufactured synthetic crystals with the property of generating a minute particle of light when struck by ionizing radiation. It had taken Kewanee 16 years to perfect its processes, and the company regarded several of the processes—the purification of raw material, the growth of the crystals, and the preparation and encapsulation of the crystals—as trade secrets which gave it a competitive advantage over its competitors. It is customary in the synthetic crystal industry to use both patents and trade secrets. (It has been noted in Chapter 3, that certain industries normally employ trade secrets when they suspect that patent infringement will be difficult to prove.) All of Kewanee's employees were required to sign employment agreements promising not to disclose confidential information or trade secrets. Subsequently, four of the company's employees resigned and formed the defendant Bicron Corporation, which within nine months was marketing a competing product.

In the trial court the plantiff claimed that all of its processes were secret. The defendants not only argued that the plaintiff had failed to maintain the proper security required to protect a trade secret, but also that each of the claimed secrets was not, in fact, a trade secret but rather industrial know-how. The District Court came out squarely in the middle: it decided what was secret and what was not and then issued an injunction against the disclosure of the trade secrets but refused to enjoin the defendants from the use of the industrial know-how. In the best of worlds, the distinction between secrets that are confidential and know-how that is presumed to be public is rarely clear-cut. So both sides appealed.

A brief of amicus curiae, filed by the Association for the Advancement of Invention and Innovation, argued on behalf of the plaintiff, Kewanee, that no company embarking on an R&D program can ever be certain whether an invention will ultimately be held patentable or unpatentable. If both trade secrets and know-how are not rigorously protected, the results are likely to be the encouragement of industrial espionage, the reduction of research budgets, and the loss of a billion dollars of royalties per year under know-how license agreements. The Court of Appeals, however, determined that the principal issue was whether the federal patent laws preempt the field for patentable subject matter, thus invalidating state trade secret laws. Acknowledging that other courts had decided to the contrary,[8] it reviewed the history of patent and trade secret laws and decided that state trade secret laws, which, in effect, grant an unlimited monopoly, are in direct conflict with patent laws, which have as their purpose the objective of obtaining public disclosure after a limited period of time. The Supreme Court of the United States, however, reversed *Kewanee* stating that there is no real possibility that trade secret law will conflict with federal patent policy. The majority argued that abolition of trade secret protection would not result in increased disclosure to the public of discoveries in the area of nonpatentable subject matter. The Court stated,

Even as the extension of trade secret protection to patentable subject matter that the owner knows will not meet the standards of patentability will not conflict with the patent policy of disclosure, it will have a decidedly beneficial effect on society. Trade secret law will encourage invention in areas where patent law does not reach, and will prompt the independent innovator to proceed with the discovery and exploitation of his invention. Competition is fostered and the public is not deprived of the use of valuable, if not patentable, invention.[9]

For the time being, the status of trade secrets has been restored to an unsteady respectability.

These recent cases reflect the state of turmoil in the law regarding which forms of protection may properly be used to safeguard intellectual property without discouraging competition or unreasonably extending monopoly. What has been the reaction of industry toward patent and trade secret in an atmosphere of legal uncertainty? In the next section, industrial attitudes and behavior are examined by the project staff.

The Intellectual Property Survey

Through a combination of written questionnaires and personal interviews,[10] the project team surveyed the opinions of 552 companies about a variety of issues involving the protection of innovation through trade secrets. The survey was directed to companies in six industrial states in each of three major technical fields:

- Energy Conservation
- Public Health
- Environmental Protection

The energy field was further subdivided into three major industrial classifications: coal, electricity, and petroleum. Each of the five industrial areas was keyed to an SIC group code, and respondents were selected from Standard & Poor's 1973 Index, Dun & Bradstreet Middle Market Index for 1973, Funk & Scott 1973 Index, the 1973 Thomas Register Directory, and 1973 state manufacturing directories for all states. Sample analysis was based upon an average 10 percent reply. Table 7-2 indicates the distribution of inquiries. The number of responses varied according to the questions posed. (For present purposes, the written and oral responses are combined.)

The survey was designed to elicit answers to the following questions:

- Has there been any marked change in the number of disclosures of patentable or nonpatentable technology in the last three years?
- If a company has a trade secret policy for its employees, does it maintain an inventory of trade secrets?
- Do trade secrets describe inventions that would otherwise be patentable?
- Do companies employ any mode of protection other than patent or trade secret?
- In the context of a company's business, is one legal form of protecting intellectual property regarded as superior to another?
- Has the company ever been involved in litigation over proprietary rights?
- If other economic and technical factors are equal, does the availability of protection for intellectual property affect the utilization of innovations?
- Is the development of any products or processes believed to have been frustrated by deficiencies in the law of intellectual property?
- Is the development of any products or processes believed to have been frustrated by legal deficiencies other than in the laws of intellectual property?

Tables 7-3 and 7-4 indicate the size of the companies participating in the survey. As measured by either sales volume or number of employees, it is apparent that most of the survey respondents were large corporations. The respondents in the energy conservation category were principally the energy

Table 7-2
Intellectual Property Survey Distribution of Inquiries

State	Energy Conservation			Public Health	Environmental Protection	Total
	Coal	Electricity	Petroleum			
California	7	11	34	35	14	101
Illinois	13	27	9	17	13	79
Massachusetts	0	0	0	19	2	21
New York	15	13	49	36	21	134
Pennsylvania	70	27	15	11	18	141
Texas	3	58	15	0	9	85
Total	108	136	122	118	77	561

Table 7-3

Size of Respondent Measured by Total Annual Sales Volume and Volume of Sales in Goods or Services Involved in Survey (Figures represent percentage of respondents within each sales category)

Sales	Energy Conservation						Public Health		Environmental Protection	
	Coal		Electricity		Petroleum					
	T^a	S^b	T	S	T	S	T	S	T	S
Over $50 million	.67	.67	.71	.64	.71	.79	.50	.40	.67	.33
$5 - $50 million	.11	.11	0	.07	.21	.14	.10	.20	0	.25
$1 - $5 million	.22	.11	.14	.14	0	0	.30	.30	.17	.25
$500,000 - $1 million	0	0	.14	.14	0	0	.10	0	.17	.17
$100,000 - $500,000	0	.11	0	0	.07	.07	0	.10	0	0
Number of companies	10		14		14		10		12	

[a]Total annual sales volume.
[b]Volume of sales in goods or services involved in survey.

Table 7-4

Size of Respondent Measured by Number of Employees (Figures represent percentage of respondents within each employment category)

Employees	Energy Conservation			Public Health	Environmental Protection
	Coal	Electricity	Petroleum		
Over 1,000	.89	.71	.71	.50	.67
500 - 1,000	0	0	.07	0	0
100 - 500	0	0	.14	.20	0
25 - 100	.11	.14	.07	.20	.33
Less than 25	0	.14	0	.10	0

producers and distributors themselves. Understandably, virtually all of the companies regarded their sales as related to energy "conservation." The 14-company petroleum group included the country's 8 largest producers and only one refinery with sales of under half a million dollars. The 14-company electrical energy group included 9 producer-distributors and five manufacturers. The 10-company coal group included one subsidiary of an oil company, 4 steel companies, a copper company, and a chemical company. All in the 12-company environmental protection group were manufacturers. Their products ranged from chemicals to mine safety appliances. The 10-company medical instrumentation (public health) group was the only one that included several smaller companies. The conclusions relating to this group, but not the statistical analyses in this section, were modified by information obtained from interviews with three small instrumentation companies conducted for the patent part of the study.

With reference to the total survey, 63 percent of the respondents were in the various energy categories, 20 percent in the environmental protection category, and 17 percent in public health. The participation of the energy group and of seven large companies in the environmental protection group biased the survey heavily in the direction of expressing the attitudes of big business. (Fifty-seven percent of the respondents had annual sales of over $50 million, and 68 percent of them had over 1,000 employees.)

In few periods of recent industrial history has the degree of uncertainty about the various laws of intellectual property been so high. There is a general feeling among the survey respondents that legal uncertainty is a negative influence on innovation. However, in spite of this quandry, as will be seen below, the number of disclosures of innovations in recent years has remained relatively constant. Even so, a majority, albeit not a substantial majority (53 percent to 45 percent), of the sample felt that if other economic and technical factors are equal, the availability of protection for intellectual property affects the utilization of innovations developed by the company. This answer was undoubtedly influenced by the fact that many of the respondents were the patent attorneys for their companies. No professional person wants to feel that his profession has little to do with the outcome of events.[11] Nevertheless, assuming the accuracy of the insights, it is evident that either all factors are never equal, or that utilization considerations do not affect the level of innovation. Measuring innovation over the past three years by the number of disclosures of patentable and nonpatentable technology, 64 percent of the total sample felt that there had been no observable trend toward increase or diminution. Of those who felt that there had been change, only 13 percent thought that the number of disclosures had decreased and 18 percent felt that there had been a relative increase. (The replies to the question regarding number of disclosures are broken down by participant categories in Table 7-5.)

A large majority of the participants—71 percent—have active patent policies.

Table 7-5
Perception of Change in Disclosure Rate (Figures represent percentage of respondents answering under each category)

Industry	More	Same	Less
Coal	.11	.67	.22
Electricity	.21	.64	0
Petroleum	.21	.57	.21
Public Health	.20	.60	.20
Environmental Protection	.08	.67	.16

Of those who do not have such programs, the electrical distributing companies composed more than half of the respondents. On the other hand, 36 percent of the petroleum companies had well over 1,000 active patents. Among the companies with active patent programs, there was general consistency in the replies pertaining to the number of technical disclosures of all kinds and the number of patent applications filed in recent years. Fifty-five percent of the companies with active programs indicated no change in the number of patent applications filed, 25 percent reported an increase, and 20 percent reported a decrease. However, the spread by participant categories, shown in Table 7-6, reveals a significant finding. Although no group has had a positive decline in patent applications, among the petroleum and coal companies that replied to this question the percentage of companies that reported a decrease in patent applications outnumbered those who reported an increase, and the percentage of companies reporting no change was the same as that reporting a decrease. Only in public health and environmental protection was there substantial stability in patent filings.

It would appear that in some industries the number of disclosures has been increasing at a greater rate than the number of patent applications. Several possible reasons include (1) a change in the quality or type of disclosures; (2) a lack of faith in the patent system, which reduces the rate of filing; (3) a switch from patents to trade secrets if the technology so allows; (4) a decision to suppress new technology, or at least to postpone its development.

Since 78 percent of the entire sample had trade secret policies for their employees, and not a single company reported a decrease in the rate of trade secret accumulation in the past three years, the project staff attempted to put some dimensions on the second of the above possible reasons. The evidence suggests that most companies have adopted employee trade secret policies to ensure the loyalty of their employees rather than to encourage trade secrets disclosures. Only 31 percent of the sample bothers to keep an inventory of secrets at all. Of those that do, the only group with a significant showing was the public health category: 50 percent of those respondents not only keep an

Table 7-6

Change in Rate of Filing Patent Applications (1970-1973) (Figures represent percentage of respondents answering under each category)

Industry	No Change	Increased	Decreased
Coal	.33	.22	.33
Electricity	.29	.29	0
Petroleum	.29	.21	.29
Public Health	.60	.20	.20
Environmental Protection	.75	0	.16

inventory of trade secrets, but all of them reported that their trade secrets might otherwise be patentable.

Among the other groups responding to this line of questioning, roughly two thirds claimed that the subject matter of their trade secrets might be patentable. Virtually all participants who keep an inventory of trade secrets regard them to be an effective means of protecting intellectual property. Although only a 42 percent minority reported that they protect intellectual property in any manner other than patent or trade secret—the references were principally to copyright and trademark—most companies were unable to generalize about the superiority of one mode of protection over another. One large electrical engineering company reported a deliberate policy of coordinating patent and trade secret protection. Another, interviewed prior to the Supreme Court reversal of *Kewanee*, said that it regarded the two modes as overlapping, but was then uncertain. On the other hand, a large company in the environmental protection category, with an unusually sophisticated patent department, reported that they do not regard patents and trade secrets as overlapping forms of protection.

Forty-nine percent of the sample had been involved in proprietary rights litigation at one time or another. One large oil company, with a portfolio of over 2,000 patents, noted that in the past decade the number of suits involving theft of trade secrets and breach of confidence has been rising relative to classical infringement actions. Another oil company, which depends heavily on trade secrets to protect its blending formulations, has simply become diligent in protecting them from many of its own employees.

It has been observed above that 53 percent of the respondents felt that the availability of protection affects the utilization of innovations, while 45 percent felt it does not make any difference. The distribution of responses was approximately the same in all five participating industrial categories. Although most of the large oil companies related their affinitive response to the importance of royalty income, the others who stressed the importance of protection invariably said that their companies would be reluctant to invest in new technologies in its absence. In this regard, several companies in the environmental protection market were especially emphatic: one felt that the "compulsory licensing" features of the 1970 amendment to the Clean Air Act were counter-productive.[12] Another pointed out that the ease of infringement in water treatment plants makes patents essential to justify investment in research.

The 45 percent that were unable to relate legal protection to utilization included several companies that are universally regarded as innovative. Their view was that innovation is an essential part of market strategy. They seek all the protection they can get, but its absence will not affect innovation if they can acquire a market lead and if there is a reasonable promise of profits. Many of the companies in both groups expressed concern about the possible effect of the then pending *Kewanee* case; all of the participants desired patent reform to reduce the proportion of patents invalidated on appeal.

It is not an all-or-nothing proposition with either group. Considering that 85 percent of the total sample could not recall the development of any product or process having been frustrated because of the law of intellectual property, it would seem that on this issue the attitude of the 45 percent minority is more consistent with actual industrial behavior than that of the majority. Figure 7-1 is a categorized breakdown of responses regarding the effect of the law of intellectual property on research and development.

One could conclude from the variance between expressed dissatisfaction with the law of intellectual property and the fact that industrial development proceeds apace, either that the dissatisfaction is overstated, or that this body of law is simply not influential. Evidence that the latter conjecture is closer to the truth arises out of industrial response when the scope of the inquiry is expanded from the law of intellectual property to all law. When asked whether industrial development has, in fact, been frustrated by other laws, the affirmative responses were more than doubled (from 15 percent to 35 percent). Although 67 percent of the sample still felt that legal deficiencies did not frustrate industrial development, one out of every three companies felt otherwise. Moreover, this time the categorical spread was sensitive to industry size. The petroleum group, which contains the largest companies, is less sensitive to the influence of the law on development than the medical instrumentation group, which includes a few smaller concerns. (The categorical breakdown is set forth in Figure 7-2.) The other laws most often mentioned by the medical instrumentation companies involved FDA approvals and the title policy of the government in federally sponsored research.

In general, the project staff found a high correlation between the responses of

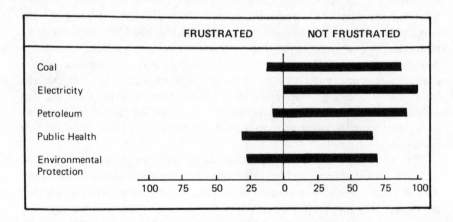

Figure 7-1. Amount of R&D Believed to Have Been Frustrated by Intellectual Property Laws

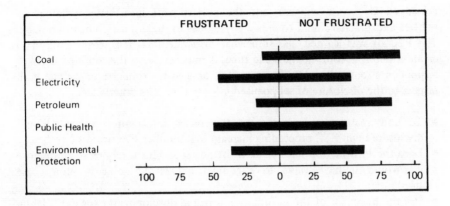

Figure 7-2. Amount of R&D Believed to Have Been Frustrated by Other Laws

the companies surveyed for this study (both the responses of the 60 companies in the intellectual property survey and the more detailed interview results of the patent section) and the industrial attitudes toward patents published in the earlier Government Patent Policy Study.

Government Solicitation of Trade Secrets: The Federal Trade Commission

The trade secret is under attack from all sides: the lower courts questions the very legitimacy of the concept in both *Lear* and *Kewanee*. Executive agencies that sponsor research and development retain title to data (including trade secrets) unless it is developed entirely at private expense, properly marked, and brought to the attention of the contracting officer.[13] One major regulatory agency, the Federal Trade Commission, even has the statutory authority to subpoena commercial and industrial trade secrets in order to enforce unfair competition laws.[14] Although the statute itself forbids the publication of confidential information subpoenaed by the agency, the courts have ruled that there is no absolute protection for trade secrets; their disclosure may be properly required if the information is relevant to the issues in an adjudicative proceeding.[15] In the absence of a court order, however, FTC employees, as well as other federal employees, are prohibited from revealing confidential proprietary information under the threat of a criminal sanction in the general criminal statutes.[16]

The Commission has a substantial interest in soliciting secrets that have been developed at private expense, and the project staff investigated whether its policies and practices tend to create any blocks to the utilization of technology. The FTC, it was learned, has somewhat of a dilemma. It is legally obliged to create a public record; at the same time, it must preserve the confidentiality of respondents' data. Accordingly, it has felt obliged to formalize its criteria with respect to the disclosure of subpoenaed information. The criteria are:

- To how many people is the putative secret information known? Would disclosure in an FTC proceeding increase that number significantly?
- Does the information have value to its posessor who is requested to disclose it? Would it have value to a competitor? Is the value in either case substantial?
- Has the possessor of the information incurred development expenses? Has he realized a return on them?
- What damage, if any, would the possessor suffer from the disclosure sought? What advantages might his competitors derive from such disclosure?
- Would any benefits be derived from disclosure? And if so, to whom? Specifically, is there a public "need" justifying disclosure? Is the need significant? Could it be satisfied without disclosure?

The balancing of equities, implicit in the FTC criteria, is substantially at variance with the trade secret concept accepted by industry and by research-sponsoring federal agencies. This arises partly because the so-called "trade secrets" with which the FTC normally deals are more in the nature of confidential commercial data, with a smattering of industrial know-how, than technological innovations. For example, in the *Chock Full o'Nuts Corp., Inc.*, case,[17] the respondent argued that recipies for coffee, baked goods, and so forth, were trade secrets.[18] In addition to the culinary specifications, the data the respondent requested the Commission to hold confidential included a substantial amount of franchising information relating to alleged tie-in sales. The issue in the case was whether Chock could compel its licensees to purchase its foodstuffs, prepared according to "secret" processes, as well as particular branded goods. The Commission ordered the respondent to desist from forcing its franchisees to purchase food products from suppliers other than Chock. It could continue to compel them to purchase coffee and baked goods that it manufactured itself according to its secret recipes. The FTC did not reveal the recipes—this time. One as yet unresolved issue is whether or not a formula replicable by reverse engineering (even at great expense) should be granted trade secret status. The FTC is inclined toward a negative answer because of its obligation to create a public record.

A review of many of the pending cases and discussion with FTC counsel convinced the project staff that the Commission is sensitive to the possibility that its trade secret policies could act as a barrier to innovation regarding commercially profitable consumer products. It should be noted, however, that the Commission has yet to face a difficult decision in an area *of high technology.* Its current litigation is principally involved with cornflakes, coffee, hamburgers, and the like. However, it is highly probable that in the near future the FTC will wish to investigate practices in a high technology field where the forefront of science may be involved. The Commission's evolving philosophy of the protection of trade secrets does not support the hope that the FTC will then be as concerned with the utilization of technology as it is with insuring competition and preventing monopoly. Even so, there is little in the record of the Antitrust Division cases or the intellectual property survey discussed above to indicate that industrial utilization would be appreciably affected one way or the other. The statement of the FTC's Director of the Bureau of Competition that there is a "complete lack of empirical evidence that antitrust is a bar to technological development"[19] is probably a self-serving prediction.

8 Copyright and Data

Introduction

It is generally assumed that the pace of technological innovation, and hence the utilization of technology, is influenced by the systems, laws, and regulations that govern the accessibility and movement of knowledge from one part of society to another. Copyright law involves a simple system of registration without examination. A singular feature of patent law, on the other hand, is a complex (and expensive) examination system. Accordingly, it is usually supposed that copyright law presents fewer barriers to the utilization of technology—to the extent that it is involved with technology at all. Interestingly, it so happened that for 43 years (from 1793 to 1836) the patent system was also a registration system.[1] A patent was granted to anyone who applied, submitted the proper drawings, and paid a fee. In 1836, however, examination for novelty, utility, and invention were reinstated, thus sharply delineating patent and copyright.

Our investigation of whether copyright (and data regulations) do, in fact, influence technological utilization was addressed to two questions: Do existing provisions of coyyright law or the data and publication regulations of the federal government inhibit technological utilization? Or, conversely, do current practices for making data available from the federal government promote utilization? Our research in this area focused primarily on a survey of the computer software industry and also on the administrative policies of the National Aeronautics and Space Administration and the National Technical Information Service, both of which are actively involved in the dissemination of technical information at the federal level. We will first discuss special questions surrounding the status accorded computer programs as a form of intellectual property and current attitudes on modes of protecting software. Patent and data promotion and licensing policies of NASA and NTIS will then be described.

Protection of Computer Software

The protection of intellectual property in the computer software industry is a special case. A multimillion-dollar industry, given special impetus, as noted in Chapter 5, by the so-called "unbundling" decision,[2] its technical output is denied patent protection as a matter of law.[3] Lacking access to patents for all practical purposes (one of the rare patents issued in this field has allegedly been infringed by a government agency), the computer software industry relies on other legal and physical techniques of safeguarding proprietary rights. Yet there has been a question as to the relative effectiveness of the various other techniques. For example, although the U.S. Copyright Office accepts registration for copyright of computer programs,[4] over a period of nine years (through 1972) there have been only 750 such registrations. The current annual rate is 125 to 150 per year (as compared with roughly 168,000 registrations in the entire "books" class, where they are placed).

In its investigation of the protection of computer software, the project staff enlisted the cooperation of the Association of Data Processing Service Organizations (ADAPSO) to poll its membership on the types of legal protection used for software, the relative satisfaction with the available modes of protection, and whether legal barriers are ever instrumental in discouraging or preventing the development or marketing of software. Thirty-one of the 46 companies polled responded to the ADAPSO questionnaire. Members of the project staff attended the annual meeting of the Association and had the opportunity to discuss the subject matter of the questionnaire with individual respondents. Although the legal protection of software is the subject of many articles, treatises, and conferences, to the best of our knowledge this is the first empirical study of the subject.

Like the industry itself, ADAPSO is a relatively young organization. All except one of the 31 firms responding are under 11 years old. Most of the companies (87 percent) are independently owned. In almost all cases, the president or vice president of the company answered the questionnaire. Table 8-1 presents a profile of respondents by sales volume and number of employees.

The respondents provide a variety of services in the software field, as shown in Figure 8-1, with nearly all firms offering proprietary software packages. None of the firms surveyed manufacture hardware or peripheral equipment. More than half of the respondents (58 percent) stated that over 50 percent of their sales volume is related to the development and sale of computer software as an end product, and most of this sales volume is in proprietary software. (Fifty-two

Table 8-1
Profile of ADAPSO Respondents (Figures indicate percentage of respondents in each category)

Sales		Number of Employees	
Over $50 million	.03	Above 1,000	.07
$5 to $50 million	.10	500 to 1,000	0
$1 59 $ 5 million	.42	100 to 500	.13
$500,000 to $1 million	.16	25 to 100	.45
$100,000 to $500,000	.29	Under 25	.35

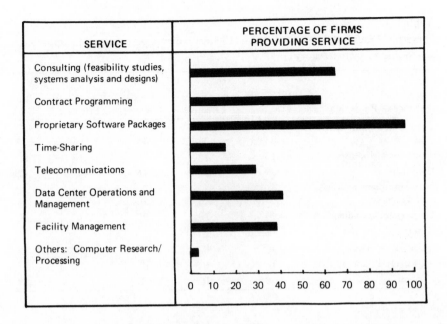

Figure 8-1. Types of Services Provided

percent of the firms attributed more than half their sales volume to proprietary software, while the same percentage stated that less than 10 percent of total volume comes from programs developed at the customer's expense.)

The preferred modes of legal protection for proprietary software are shown in Table 8-2. No method of safeguarding software is regarded as completely effective by all respondents. Thirty-five percent of the respondents regard the lease as very effective, and 26 percent of those who use copyright find it somewhat effective. In cases where respondents designated a particular protection technique as not at all effective, they were asked to explain their answer in terms of their actual business experience. Of the 10 comments received, two companies stated that the cost of litigation and legal advice makes protection of rights impracticable. (These were infringement situations—one patent and one copyright.) Several qualified their "ineffective" ranking to mean they had made a business decision not to go the "protection" route, or that the techniques seem impracticable (except for confidential disclosure clauses). One company felt it needed more protection, although it had had no specific problems. Other comments were that limiting access is ineffective when trying to sell to outside users, that lack of knowledge of copyright principles inhibits the use of this technique, and that any program may be "dumped" from memory with sufficient decoding of the object program to make the inspection of techniques incorporated relatively simple.

Table 8-2

Preferred Modes of Legal Protection (Figures indicate percentage of respondents answering in each category)

	Degree of Effectiveness				
Mode of Protection	Not At All Effective	Somewhat Effective	Very Effective	Completely Effective	Not Used
Lease with a Confidential Disclosure	.03	.23	.35	.16	.23
Trade Secret License	.13	.16	.26	.10	.35
Copyright	.09	.26	.16	.07	.42
Physically Limiting Access to Technology	.07	.16	.20	.13	.44
Cryptographic Coding	.13	.10	.07	0	.70
Other:					
Software Lock	0	0	.08	0	.97
Controlled Support	0	0	.03	0	.97
Patent	.03	0	0	0	.97

The companies' use and perception of the effectiveness of protection techniques appear to be moderately correlatable to several outside variables.[5] Of those tested (annual sales, number of employees, derivation of sales from proprietary or contract software), no single variable has a very marked relationship with the survey responses. However, taken together, the outside variables tested showed a correlation index between .30 and .60. Thus, although the correlations are not that significant individually, they do indicate as a group that the responses to questions about use and perceived effectiveness of techniques are tied in to certain company characteristics: as sales, number of employees, or percentage of sales attributable to programming increases, the use and perceived effectiveness of various protection techniques also increases.

As shown in Table 8-3, protection is regarded as most significant for general business and financial operations, and for systems software (for example, new techniques for more efficient processing or machine utilization).

Opinions about the significance of software protection in different application areas seem, for the most part, to be held randomly throughout the sample. Specifically, the low correlations found when crossing this question with sales level, number of employees, and types of services provided suggest that opinions regarding software protection are not significantly affected by outside variables. Only one variable seemed to correlate even moderately with opinions on software protection. The figures show a slight positive correlation (.50) between sales derivation and software protection opinions for general business and financial applications. Those companies with a higher percentage of sales from contract software placed greater significance on software protection for

Table 8-3

Significance of Software Protection by Function (Figures indicate percentage of respondents answering in each category)

Function	No Significance	Some Significance	Great Significance	NA
General Business and Financial Applications (accounting, inventory control, payroll)	.19	.26	.42	.13
Business Planning Operations (planning models, simulations, operations research)	.29	.13	.29	.29
Complex Production/Distribution Control Operations (linear programming)	.35	.19	.10	.35
Engineering and Scientific Applications	.32	.16	.13	.39
Data and Statistical Analysis	.26	.29	.13	.31
Project Management and Control	.29	.36	.03	.32
Systems Software (compilers, monitors, new techniques for more efficient machine utilization)	.16	0	.62	.22

general business and financial applications. With respect to systems software applications, however, this relation did not hold. There was only a negligible correlation (.08) between sales attributable to proprietary software and software protection for general business and financial applications.

Eighty-seven percent of all respondents could not think of a single instance in which computer programs representing a significant level of innovation were not developed or marketed because of inadequate protection.[6] The four companies that thought the law had been a barrier cited examples in which fear of easy plagiarism or unauthorized disclosure might prevent recoupment of development costs. The situations cited involved such techniques as paging programs for virtual memory computers, an innovative approach to developing multiprogramming capability on the IBM 360/20, and systems software for organizing computer program libraries. Most interesting, perhaps, was the disclosure at the ADAPSO meeting that the mode of protecting intellectual property (that is, computer software) is as likely to be governed by a desired characterization for tax purposes as it is for safeguarding or transferring technology. This is because intellectual property protected by patent or copyright may be subject to local property taxes, and can be capitalized for federal income tax purposes, while intellectual property (the existence of which is not a matter of record) is not readily made a subject of taxation.

Active Data Utilization Policies

The practices of two government agencies are of particular interest with respect to our discussion of the laws of copyright and data. This section describes the policies of the National Aeronautics and Space Administration (NASA) and the National Technical Information Service (NTIS), their relation to legal modes of protection of intellectual property, and to the utilization of technology.

NASA's technology utilization program, which is as old as the agency itself, has new vigor under the impetus of a challenge to justify its continued existence by proving the earthly benefits of its research. NASA requires a full invention disclosure from its contractors even if the concept has never been reduced to practice. Since 1962, the agency has screened 30,000 disclosures, filed patent applications on 2,475 inventions, and published "tech briefs" on most of the other technologies. Moreover, unlike private industry, NASA publishes its patent applications.[7] Prior to the 1971 Memorandum of Government Patent Policy, NASA applied for a patent only if there was a government use for the invention. Now, however, it will file on any disclosure with a potential commercial application.

The recent policy of the agency has been to grant nonexclusive licenses only to applicants who are likely to utilize the invention. The term of the license may be less than that of the patent. If it is found that the invention is not being worked by a nonexclusive licensee, and if the invention is not in a class in which the government must retain title under the Memorandum, then NASA will grant an exclusive license in order to promote utilization. However, the license is revocable if the patent is not worked. The licensee is entitled to sue to enjoin infringement, and the agency reserves the right to join in the action. The government also reserves the right to impose field-of-use limitations to retain public health and safety features in the public domain. The program is, or was, sufficiently sophisticated with respect to utilization that it often insisted on a minimum investment before granting an exclusive license and also offered exclusive licenses to foreign licensees who would work the patent in the United States. Now, however, it is not at all certain how much of NASA's program will remain intact since *Public Citizen v. Samson.*[8]

The conversion from a passive to an active utilization policy required the NASA Technology Utilization Office to create or find new institutions to promote technology.[9] It assisted in the creation of, and generally supports by contract, six regional application centers for technical data and patented technology.[10] Basically, the centers are computer terminals manned by full-time employees (called "interface men") who access government technological data banks for industrial clients.

The information on the computer tapes comes principally from NASA, although it is also supplied by the Department of Defense and other trade and educational resources. A customer pays an annual subscription fee to the application center, which entitles him to establish a contact point within his company. There is no limit to the number of probes by the contact point. The interface man analyzes the customer's technical inquiry, translates the inquiry into machine-readable language, and delivers copies of technical documents bearing upon the question posed. The customer can continue to receive update information as long as he wants it and is willing to pay for it. The charge is for the service; there is no charge for the data.

In addition to the NASA data banks, the Centers have access to, and expect to tie in to, the growing central technology data banks of the Department of Commerce's National Technical Information Service in Springfield, Virginia. Although the patent rather than the data package has traditionally been the linch-pin of the NASA utilization program, it is not clear whether the users are interested in the licenses or in the technical information in the patent specifications. In any event, the fact that 200 industrial customers are already paying at least $1,700 each for data accessed by the New England Regional Application Center alone, and the high attendance and level of interest at the NASA regional patent licensing conferences, augur well for its active utilization program.

An agency of the Department of Commerce, the National Technical Information Service (NTIS) was established as a central source for the public sale of government-sponsored research, development, and engineering reports and other analyses prepared by federal agencies, their contractors, or their grantees. Its mission, in effect, is to remove barriers to utilization both by collecting technical information at a central point and by improving access to it. The NTIS collection exceeds 730,000 titles, and more than 100,000 documents are currently in stock.

Two aspects of NTIS operations are particularly worthy of note. First, there is no law or regulation that requires federal agencies to file reports and documents with NTIS (to the presumed end of making their existence known and contents available). The agency, accordingly, works out a modus operandi with each agency. Some have standing orders that all technical reports will be filed at NTIS; others do not. Second, the agency is required by statute to recover its costs, and only a small portion of its total expenditures are covered by congressional appropriation. The Government Printing Office (GPO), on the other hand, is more heavily subsidized by Congress and can thus offer some kinds of documents to the public at a lower price than NTIS.

One question presented to the NTIS staff was whether they were aware of any complaints that the regulations of government agencies served as a barrier to innovation by inhibiting the flow of information. For example, were they aware of any alleged abuses of discretionary authority under the Freedom of Information Act? We were unable to identify, in these discussions, any current or recent specific situation where such regulations or policies allegedly erect a barrier in a specific area of technology. From the nature of the question posed, of course, it is clear that the result is by no means conclusive; a very effective barrier could result not only in nondissemination, but nonawareness as well.

NTIS did point out one prevalent practice that might diminish the general level of available information, but it is difficult to assess its final impact on innovation. Many federal agencies prefer to publish through the Government Printing Office rather than NTIS. This preference is based on the premise that GPO, because of its lower cost structure, will reach a wider audience. (It may be, too, that GPO is better known than NTIS.) NTIS argues that GPO should not be the sole distribution agency, for two reasons: (1) GPO will often discontinue an item when sales drop off, so that eventually there are no copies available and (2) NTIS has a superior indexing/accessing system. NTIS also points out that many people mistakenly believe that GPO publishes all government documents that are in the public domain.

On the narrower issue of whether copyright restrictions present a barrier to utilization, NTIS does have problems, but not to the extent that any inhibiting effect on utilization can be documented. The agency operates on the general assumption that work performed under government contracts is in the public domain. Accordingly, when a report is received with a contractor copyright claim, NTIS queries the originating agency as to the validity of the claim and, if valid, attempts to obtain from the copyright owner an authorization to reproduce. The end result is some delay, but there is no evidence that the delay significantly inhibits utilization.[11]

According to NTIS, many government agencies keep no systematic inventory of reports or published works that stem from contract or research grants. Again, the prevailing attitude within these agencies, as reported by NTIS, seems to be that if anything worthwhile results from research, it will eventually—say, within 12 to 18 months after completion—find its way into a scholarly journal or other publication. The above observations pertain to the present situation, where NTIS is dealing principally with reports that are in (or should be in) the public domain, and where reproductions are available, either in microfilm or hard copy, upon placement of an order. Taking the long-term view, there is a way in which copyright law can erect a very real barrier to technological innovation. Here we are talking about the "information dissemination" industry itself and the shape it is likely to take in the decades ahead.

As noted earlier in this report, technology has outstripped copyright law. In the view of many observers, we may no longer be talking about modifications to eliminate undesirable side effects in an essentially sound system, but about fundamental changes in the system itself. The question has been given thoughtful consideration by the COSATI Panel on Legal Aspects of Information Systems.[12] The Panel acknowledged two fundamental hypotheses that are engrained in our societal values and on which the copyright law has been built:

- The creator should receive compensation for the use by others of his creative product or as a reward for creation.
- Society as a whole should have the maximum possible access to the creative products of its members.

In the view of the Panel, the intrinsic conflict between these hypotheses gives rise to serious issues that are aggravated by the information revolution. Given the present state of technology, we can visualize a nationwide information network that could make available to educational institutions, large libraries, and businesses newly created knowledge as well as past work—for example, the contents of the Library of Congress. Basically, such a system involves the transmission of information by electronic means and with reasonably prompt access at a multitude of remote locations. If such an information network were put into actual practice, we would require drastically new legal approaches to the definition of use and to the development of equitable compensation mechanisms.

Appendixes

Appendix A: Government Patent Policy Study for the Federal Council on Science and Technology, Harbridge House, Inc., May 17, 1968

Summary and Analysis of Findings

A. Study Objectives and Approach

The primary purpose of the Harbridge House study has been to provide government policy makers with data to evaluate the effectiveness of government patent policy in achieving policy objectives. The study sought answers to three basic questions which underlie the government's objectives concerning patents arising out of government contracts:

(i) How does patent policy affect commercial utilization of government-sponsored inventions?

(ii) How does patent policy affect business competition in commercial markets?

(iii) How does patent policy affect participation of contractors in the government's research and development programs?

A three-phase study effort was undertaken to answer these questions: In phase one, existing data was gathered to determine what relevant information was already available. Phase two consisted of a utilization questionnaire survey to gather a broad body of new data on a large sample of government-sponsored inventions. And, phase three involved case studies of inventions and contractors in the utilization survey to develop a fuller understanding of the effects of patent policy on them.

The first phase involved four separate tasks. A literature search was conducted to determine what existing data were available on the study questions. In addition, three research tasks were conducted within government activities to (i) determine the promotional programs of eight government agencies; (ii) review reported instances of industry hesitation or refusal to participate in programs of the Department of Interior and the National Institutes of Health (NIH) for reasons relating to patents; and (iii) examine 100 contractor NASA waiver requests to determine the basis for waivers of patent title granted by NASA. These tasks, useful in themselves, also provided background information in conducting phases two and three of the study.

In the second phase of the study, commercial utilization of all government-sponsored inventions patented in 1957 and 1962[1] were surveyed through questionnaires[2] to gather data on utilization and li-

censing of a large and statistically significant group of patents. A two-year sample was selected to ensure against bias in patents issued in a given year, and the years 1957 and 1962 were chosen to allow enough time for sample inventions to be applied commercially. Although the sample predates the current policy established by the Kennedy Memorandum of 1963, patent rights in sample inventions were allocated in different ways under various programs making it possible to project the results of the study in terms of current policy.

Questionnaires on each invention were sent to organizations which developed them regardless whether the contractor or the government retained title. Similar questionnaires were also sent to firms which requested licenses to government-owned inventions, whether developed under contracts on in government laboratories, to compare conditions under which inventions might be used with and without exclusive rights. Both included questions on the size and business orientation of the responder; the nature of the invention; the role it played in its commercial use; the speed with which it was applied; the type and amount of private funds invested in applying it; the sales attributable to the invention; the extent to which it was available for and resulted in licenses by patentee; and the reasons for nonutilization where it was not used commercially.

Questionnaire responses were received on about 60 percent of the sample inventions and were analyzed to determine the patterns of utilization, and the effect of patent rights and other factors on commercial use, licensing and business competition. The data were also used to select areas for case research in phase three of this study.

The case research in phase three gathered more detailed data on selected government contractors and inventions to understand better the factors which control decisions to utilize government-sponsored inventions, the utilization process, the effect of utilized inventions on business competition and the factors affecting willingness of contractors to participate in government-sponsored R&D programs. Five groups of case studies were conducted:

(i) Twenty-one high and low utilizers of sample inventions were interviewed to determine the reasons for their performance.

(ii) All sample inventions of TVA, and the Department of Agriculture and Interior were

---

[1] For government agencies other than DOD, AEC and NASA all patents issued from 1956 to 1966 were included because of the small number of patents issued on inventions of those agencies in 1957 and 1962.

[2] Copies of the questionnaires are included in an appendix to this report.

investigated to determine the effect of agency mission on invention utilization.

(iii) Sixteen educational and nonprofit institutions representing a cross section of all types and sizes of organization were interviewed to determine what role they play in promoting utilization of government-sponsored inventions.

(iv) All sample inventions involved in infringement suits were investigated to identify what effect they have on business competition.

(v) An industry study involving the medicinal chemistry program of NIH was performed to determine the effect of patent policy on voluntary industry participation in, and utilization of the results of the government program.

B. Effect of Government Patent Policy on Commercial Utilization

The study sought answers to several key questions concerning commercial utilization of government-sponsored inventions. Among these were:

(i) Under what circumstances have government inventions been utilized?

(ii) How important have exclusive patent rights been in promoting their use compared with other factors such as market potential, prior experience and amount of private investment required?

(iii) Under what conditions has utilization been optimized by government ownership of patents? By contractor ownership of patents?

(iv) Has substantial private investment been required to develop government-sponsored inventions for commercial use?

(v) Has such investment been made when everyone has been free to use the invention?

Several factors were found to have an important bearing on the answers to these questions. The intended uses of the sample inventions were found to have a primary effect on their commercial potential. Their intended uses, in turn, were determined by the R&D missions of the sponsoring government agencies. Once the invention was developed, several factors were found to affect their actual use in commercial markets—the extent of market demand for products employing them, the degree of promotion by government agencies which sponsored them, the size of private investment required to apply them, the prior experience and attitude toward innovation of organizations that developed them, and the type of patent rights available to protect the user's investment in bringing the inventions to market.

These factors have had the following net effect on utilization of sample inventions:

Of 2,024 contractor inventions in the two sample years for which information was available, 251 were used commercially.

- Two hundred were utilized by industrial contractors and all but seven were owned by them. Twenty-six of these were utilized by their licensees.
- An additional 51 inventions not utilized by contractors were utilized by their licensees. Ten of these inventions were owned by educational and nonprofit institutions.
- Fifty-five played a critical role in the commercial products in which they were used.
- All but two resulted from DOD contracts.

The study also reviewed 126 government-owned inventions from all sources, in-house and contractor, patented in 1957 and 1962 for which a license was issued to firms other than the inventing contractor. Ten of 126 inventions were reported used by some 50 licensees. Utilization is concentrated in TVA and Agriculture inventions which account for 60 percent of the utilized patents and 90 percent of the commercial users.

Measured in sales, commercial utilization of the inventions studied amounted to $616 million through calendar year 1966:

- $406 million were sales by contractors who owned the inventions.
- $210 million were sales by nonexclusive government licensees.
- All but $271,000 of contractor sales were from DOD inventions.

Sales of inventions, both with and without exclusive rights, were heavily concentrated in a few patents:

- 88 percent of contractor sales where the invention played a critical role are attributable to five patents in the fields of transistors, vacuum tubes, numerical control devices, computers, and gas turbine engines.
- About half the sales of licensees are attributable to three patents on the manufacture of potato flakes.

Study inventions that were used commercially found quick application in their commercial use. About one-third were applied by the time a patent application was filed, and almost two-thirds were in use when a patent issued.

A factor instrumental in the speed of utilization is prior experience. If rapid utilization is defined as occurring within three years of application for a patent, then firms with experience achieved rapid utilization over 80 percent of the time compared with half that for firms without.

The mix of government and commercial work within a firm also has an important effect. Firms in the middle range of government activity (20 to 80 percent government business) use inventions much more quickly than companies predominantly in either the commercial or the government markets.

1. Effect of Agency Mission and Commercial Potential of Sample Inventions on Utilization

The R&D mission of the sponsoring government agency was found to have a critical effect on the commercial applicability of the sample inventions. The Department of Defense, NASA and AEC accounted for some 90 percent of contracted research and more than 98 percent of the patents arising under contract in the years under study. Inventions covered by these patents were designed to meet operating requirements of these agencies rather than civilian needs in the great majority of cases. Their commercial applications, therefore, were essentially a by-product of governmental uses and depended largely on coincidental overlap between government and commercial requirements. Thus, over 70 percent of the reasons advanced by responders as most important to nonutilization of sample inventions relate to their limited commercial potential. This in no way measures their value for their intended use, but simply indicates the effect of differences between operating requirements of the government and civilian needs in commercial markets.

On the other hand, commercial inventions with significant utilization were among the patents of these agencies in the fields of transistors, vacuum tubes, numerical control devices, computers and gas turbine engines, where the necessary commercial overlap did exist.

The sample inventions of other agencies—such as the Department of Agriculture and Interior, and TVA—were highly oriented to civilian requirements reflecting the civilian orientation of their R&D missions. Since most of the Agriculture and TVA R&D programs are conducted in-house, the sample included few inventions developed by their contract programs. However, these were supplemented with in-house inventions for which the agencies granted licenses. All that were used commercially, were used without exclusive patent rights. This was largely attributable to three factors: the commercial orientation of the inventions, good potential demand for their use, and sufficient government development of the inventions to show their commercial feasibility. Notwithstanding the commercial potential of these government inventions, agency promotion within industry was important in achieving utilization of Agriculture and TVA patents because of the need to convince firms of their commercial value. In several instances, utilizing firms acquired some measure of patent protection by

developing patentable improvement to the government inventions.

Two causes predominated in cases where the inventions of these agencies did not achieve commercial utilization. Lack of full technical development of the inventions was the most frequent and important. No market need due to the complexity of the invention, its high cost compared with other methods or the availability of more practical alternatives was second in importance. It is probable that some measure of exclusive rights might have encouraged private firms to complete technical development of some inventions not fully developed by the government where adequate demand existed to make them attractive investment opportunities.

The R&D programs of HEW and Interior illustrate still another effect of mission on utilization. The programs of these two agencies are oriented to civilian needs, but in many aspects, are directed toward basic rather than applied research. The sample inventions that have resulted from their work have not, for the most part, been sufficiently developed to prove their commercial value. However, should their inventions reach that stage in programs like water desalination, and medicinal chemistry, broad commercial utilization could reasonably be anticipated because of the strong potential demand for commercial innovations in these fields.

2. Private Development Costs

Information on private development costs required to apply sample inventions commercially was somewhat sketchy due to the age of the sample and the confidential nature of the data. But the information gathered showed significant differences in the types of costs incurred on DOD-oriented inventions (with exclusive rights owned by the contractor/utilizer in almost all cases), and civilian-oriented agency inventions (with nonexclusive licenses owned by the utilizers).

Private investment was heavily concentrated in technical development of DOD inventions. Fifty-six and eight tenths (56.8) percent of private dollars were spent for development compared with 22.7 percent for production facilities and 20.5 percent for marketing the product. In contrast, only 21.1 percent of private investment was required for technical development of civilian-agency inventions, while 52.2 percent was spent on production facilities and 26.7 percent on marketing.

The data confirms the relationships observed above between agency R&D mission and commercial potential of sample inventions. Civilian agency inventions, in general, are closer to commercial products when government development is complete than are DOD inventions.

Thus, users of civilian agency inventions assume less financial risks in applying them than users of DOD inventions. This has a bearing on the degree of patent protection that may be needed as an incentive to utilization. All other factors being equal, more protection is required where the technical costs and financial risks are greater than where they are not.

3. Patent Rights as Incentives to Commercial Utilization

The study data show that patent rights play widely different roles in the business affairs of organizations in the sample. The sharpest distinction occurs between educational and nonprofit institutions, on the one hand, who can only achieve utilization of their inventions by licensing others, and industrial firms, on the other, who can promote utilization through direct use and licensing.

Educational institutions in the past have been much more concerned with publishing the results of their research than with promoting patents that may arise from it. Today, however, schools with large government research programs are taking greater interest in their patent portfolios and are seeking through a variety of means to promote them through licenses with industry. Nonprofit research firms also view their patents as a potentially useful source of income and actively seek to license others. In both cases, the inventions must frequently arise from basic research and require substantial private development before reaching the stage where they are commercially useful. Some measure of exclusive rights appears necessary to motivate licensees to invest in the work necessary to commercialize these inventions. Where the institution has an active promotional program and the government has none, commercial utilization would appear to be promoted more effectively by permitting the institution to retain exclusive rights. Where this is not so, more individual analysis is needed to determine what allocation of rights would best foster utilization.

Industrial firms in the sample place differing weights on the need for exclusive rights in using government inventions. At one extreme were firms who rely heavily on patent rights to establish their proprietary position in commercial markets and would hesitate to invest in an invention in which they could not obtain exclusive rights. At the other, were firms so completely in the government market that they attach little or no importance to patent rights for commercial purposes. In between were firms for whom patents provide a variety of incentives. The nature and importance of these incentives to firms in the sample are outlined below.

A lack of interest in patents was characteristic of some research-oriented and manufacturing firms that do a preponderance of their business in the government aerospace and defense markets. No desire to expand into commercial markets and no mechanism for the commercialization of inventions were noted. When these firms obtain patents, their sole purpose is recognition within the company of technical competence.

In a second group of firms patents were secondary to broad technical and management competence in maintaining their position in commercial markets. Firms expressing this attitude toward patents were generally manufacturers of complex systems and technical products, such as aircrafts, jet engines, computers, or communications equipment. Although as much as 75 percent of their sales may be direct to the government, these firms frequently sell similar products to commercial markets. Inventions developed during the course of R&D activities tend to be auxiliary components and subsystems or incremental improvements to the basic product. These inventions are not as important to these companies in sustaining sales or selling new products as is the basic engineering management and production capability of the firm. New ideas and inventions are incorporated in product modifications or in new models with little consideration given to the protection offered by patent rights. Using a new idea to enhance product performance is regarded as more important than assuring that the company owns the exclusive right to use it.

A third group of firms believe that corporate ownership of patents offers flexibility in design, both in the United States and abroad (through ownership of corresponding foreign patent rights), and provides trading material for cross-licenses with competitive firms. Ownership of a patent, however, as a prerequisite for new product development is a relatively minor factor compared with market considerations and investment requirements associated with commercialization of the invention. A change in government patent policy may affect firms in this category by causing them to choose more carefully the areas in which they are willing to undertake government research. Faced with the possibility of being unable to obtain title to patents they develop, these firms may refuse to contract in research areas that would impair their operational flexibility.

A fourth group of firms actively seek ownership of patents, to establish and maintain proprietary positions in new technologies, as well as in established product areas. Invariably, however, estimates of market potential and corporate investment requirements determine which product areas are developed. The makeup of the patent portfolio may indicate the direction for product development in order to strengthen proprietary positions, but development is rarely, if ever, undertaken solely because patent protection is available. A change in government policy from license rights to title rights would limit the government-sponsored R&D activity of firms in this category because of possible conflict with company-sponsored research activities. Contract opportunities would be examined on an individual basis and, in many cases, the government might be refused.

A fifth group of firms regard patent rights as essential to their business activities, and are careful to avoid government claims or conflicts over ownership of inventions. Their policies generally lead them into one of two business patterns. In the first pattern, firms will assure corporate ownership of patents before initiating work on a government contract. They may assure ownership either by negotiating contracts that permit them to acquire title to patents on inventions they may develop, or by developing and patenting basic inventions with limited private funds and then seeking contract work in order to develop additional technical competence, push the state of the art, explore a new technology, or determine if commercial applications may begin to be drawn off. In these situations, firms deliberately select areas of government research to match their commercial interests in order to generate product ideas with commercial possibilities. New research firms with strong technical abilities and limited capital typically follow this pattern, as do specialized firms that have concentrated their business in a limited area of technology.

In the second pattern, firms consciously isolate government work from their commercial operations and pursue these activities separately. The sample firms in this category did only a small percent of their business with the government and were quite independent of it. Frequently, inventions derived from government contract work by these firms will be assigned automatically to the government to avoid title conflicts or commingling with company-sponsored R&D. In other cases, government R&D will be undertaken only in areas where there is no potential conflict with corporate proprietary objectives and in order to enhance the corporate image. The technical value of government contracts to the commercial interests of these firms is rarely considered a valuable supplement to in-house research and development.

Many diversified companies follow different patent policies in their commercial and government markets. These firms may place a strong emphasis on maintaining proprietary positions in commercial markets and express a relative lack of interest in patents arising from government work. The primary purpose of securing patents on government-sponsored research discoveries as in the case of the wholly government-oriented firms, is to provide professional recognition for technical personnel.

Lastly, an important difference was observed between the research-oriented firms doing business with DOD, NASA and AEC, and the product-oriented firms whose interests are aligned with Agriculture and TVA. The former were much more aggressive in their search for useful innovations in the work they performed than the latter who tended to rely on the results of government laboratory programs for innovations in their fields. Thus, although the food, textile, and fertilizer industries are less patent-conscious, they are also more conservative in the risks they are willing to take in applying new inventions. This accounts for the frequent need for active government promotion of Agriculture and TVA inventions even when the inventions appear to have clear commercial applications.

4. Effect of Patent Policy

Notwithstanding the varying roles assigned patent rights by the firms described above, the key questions is whether permitting them to retain exclusive rights will, on balance, promote utilization better than acquisition of title by government.

The study data indicate that the answer is yes in at least the following circumstances:

(i) Where the inventions as developed under government contracts are not directly applicable to commercial uses and the inventing contractor has commercial experience in the field of the invention. This occurs most frequently with DOD, NASA and AEC inventions. In the case of DOD, the fact that it does not actively promote commercial use of its patents is an added factor. In these instances the inventing contractor with commercial experience appears to be the logical candidate to attempt utilization either directly or by licensing others; and

(ii) Where the invention is commercially oriented but requires substantial private development to perfect it, applies to a small market, or is in a field occupied by patent sensitive firms and its market potential is not alone sufficient to bring about utilization. Inventions in this category may arise with any agency and may have had only limited government development toward a commercial application.

C. Effect of Government Patent Policy on Business Competition

To evaluate the effects of government patent policy on business competition, the study tried to answer three questions:

(i) What are the effects on competition of the acquisition of exclusive commercial rights to government-sponsored inventions?

(ii) Do they increase or decrease concentration in commercial industries?

(iii) Do they create or eliminate significant areas of market power?

In evaluating the impact of government patent policy on competition, it is important to distinguish the effects of patent policy from other effects which may result from industry participation in government programs. Competitive advantages in commercial markets may well accrue to government contractors through knowledge gained in new technologies, through sharpening of technical skills, and through government funding of R&D work, which has parallel commercial areas of interest. But these are quite separate from the advantages of owning patents to specific inventions. This study has tried to measure only the latter. And, it has tried to measure it in terms of the inventions included in the survey sample. While a broader study of the cumulative effect of government-sponsored inventions patented over several years might have provided more definitive data, we believe that the study data provides a representative and useful picture of the effects of patent policy on competition.

The study indicates that both in number of inventions utilized and in sales volume, the patents sampled appear to have had small impact on commercial markets. Although over 80 percent of both sample inventions and utilization were concentrated in 50 firms, only 55 inventions owned by contractors—2.7 percent of the sample—played a critical role in their commercial use, and five were responsible for $201 million out of the $406 million in cumulative sales attributable to contractor inventions. This utilization of critical-role contractor-owned inventions is low compared with the total sales of these firms and the industries in which they participate. Of equal importance is the fact that very few instances were reported where owners of government-sponsored inventions refused to license their patents. Only 15 inventions—less than 1 percent of the sample—involved such refusals, and these 15 refusals involved just five companies.

The study did show that government retention of title, when coupled with full development and active government promotion of inventions having high commercial potential, has promoted competition. A striking example of this is the fertilizer industry where TVA developed high-concentrate fertilizers, patented them, proved their effectiveness on pilot farms and their commercial feasibility in pilot production, and aggressively promoted their use among farmers and fertilizer manufacturers. Industry sales have increased greatly through the manufacture of these fertilizers by many small regional producers. In circumstances like these, government retention of title can be an effective spur to competition because licenses are available to all comers. But several additional factors must be present for patent policy to have this effect. It must be evident to licensees that the invention has good commercial potential. The invention must be producible in commercial quantities and marketable at a cost that is competitive with alternative product. And the risks of recouping development costs must be no greater than similar investment opportunities available to the licensee.

In most cases, government agencies have to go far beyond discovery of an invention to create these conditions. Some agencies do—as described in the Volume III report on government efforts to promote utilization of government-sponsored inventions. The Department of Agriculture, for example, has an active program of developing inventions to the point of commercial feasibility. Potato flakes and frozen orange juice are two of its well-known successes. That agency in promoting potato flakes, sponsored pilot production of the product and performed a market study in supermakets in a major city to determine the product's consumer appeal. The study was then made available to the food industry to stimulate interest in the product.

In other cases, allowing industry to retain title to inventions has promoted competition. The clearest example of this is the small firm which penetrates a market of large competitors on the strength of a patent on a government sponsored invention. Just such a case is described in Volume IV, Part V, Section C.

Notwithstanding the utilization programs employed by government agencies, none except AEC has an express statutory mission to increase business competition in commercial markets for its own sake. When it does occur, however, it is an indirect result of their efforts to accomplish their basic mission. From our observations of the study inventions and insofar as the effect of patent policy is involved, competition does not appear to have been adversely affected by this lack of direct concern, for three reasons:

(i) The rate of utilization of government inventions has been low.

(ii) The agencies—such as TVA and Agriculture, whose inventions are most likely to be utilized—either developed them in-house or took title to them when developed under contract.

(iii) And industrial owners of government-sponsored inventions have been willing to license them upon request or, where they were unwilling to license, alternative technologies were available to competitors in the great majority of cases.

Based on all observations of the sample inventions we have found little evidence of adverse effects on business competition by permitting contractors to retain title of government-sponsored inventions.

D. Effect of Government Patent Policy on Industry Participation in Government R&D Programs

The effect of government patent policy on industry participation in R&D programs was the most difficult factor to measure because of the difficulty of obtaining data on the question. However, a useful understanding of problems in this area was obtained by studying the medicinal chemistry program of the National Institutes of Health (HEW) and various contracts of the Department of the Interior. This aspect of the study attempted to answer such questions as:

(i) Do competent business organizations refuse to undertake government R&D work—either entirely or in selected areas—because of government patent policy?

(ii) What effect does policy have on application of a contractor's most advanced private technology to government programs?

(iii) Does patent policy have any influence on the flow of information concerning new developments between a contractor's government and privately sponsored work?

The data available to us only allows us to define some first-order effects of the policy in this area.

Industry's main concern about participating in government research has been the compromise of private investment in research and invention. Frequent objection was made to the "peephole" effect of government programs, whereby the government receives rights in the accumulated results of private work. The "peephole" effect has its counterpart in patent matters where an invention has been conceived at private expense, but reduced to practice under a government program. The traditional patent provisions classify this as a government invention and dispose of its rights under the terms of the contract.

The reach of the contract has been extended in some program to background patents owned by the contractor at the time of contracting. This practice causes the sharpest industry reaction of all because firms feel caught between their wish to participate in government programs and the need to protect their private investment and competitive position.

The major adverse effects of patent policy on participation are program delay, loss of participants, diversion of private funds from government lines of research, and refusal to use government inventions and research when questions regarding a company's proprietary position are raised. These adverse effects occur selectively, but they have occurred at important points in government programs observed in the study.

The key to the participation questions, however, lies in the attitude of prospective contractors toward the role of patents in their activities. As noted in connection with utilization, patents have varying importance to organizations doing business with the government. Industrial firms whose major business objective is participation in government work and systems-oriented companies in the study sample were at one end of the scale and were found to assign patents a secondary role compared with technical and management competence. Patents typically were used by the former to provide recognitition to technical personnel and to project the creative quality of their work to their government customers. Systems firms, on the other hand, were found to rely on patents to ensure design freedom, provide material for cross licensing agreements as well as to recognize creativity in their technical personnel. The data indicates that firms in these two categories are not likely to refuse to participate in government R&D for patent reasons. However, systems firms may encounter participation problems at the subcontract level if the government acquires title to all inventions developed under its program.

On the other hand, firms which place a high value on patents for defensive purposes tend to choose among the areas in which they are willing to undertake government research and may decline to participate in programs which impair their operational flexibility. And, firms in research-intensive industries like electronics and new technically-oriented firms seeking to develop a proprietary product-line through government research were found to rely on patents to establish proprietary positions. These firms tend to be selective in their government-sponsored research and may decline to participate in programs which conflict with their privately sponsored research and development or which do not promote their growth objectives for proprietary lines.

Firms which follow this policy even more fully try to assure corporate ownership of patents before initiating work on a government contract or may consciously isolate government work from their commercial operations. In the latter case, there is usually little interchange of technical innovations between the government and commercial activities of the firm and there may be some loss of relevant technical experience and applications to the government work.

Lastly, large diversified firms often follow different patent policies in different divisions of the organization. Accordingly, they may be willing to participate in government programs with small concern for patents in some areas but with great concern for patent rights in others. It is difficult to generalize about these firms except to notice that their policies tend to follow the patterns of the industries in which their divisions participate. Their behavior may, therefore, resemble any of the categories of firms described above if their divisions have similar business profiles.

With respect to educational and nonprofit institutions refusal to participate for patent reasons is not normally a problem. However, instances were found in Department of Interior programs where patent problems were encountered because of conflicting institutional obligations arising from joint support of a research program or where rights in background patents were sought as a condition of the project. With the rising interest in nonprofit institutions in patents as a source of revenue, greater concern over patent rights can be expected from institutions with large research programs as financial pressures on these organizations continue to increase.

Viewing the participation problem from the standpoint of individual government agencies, the effect of patent policy varies with the nature of their R&D programs and the contractors that participate in them. Participation problems are not a concern to TVA which performs virtually all its research and development itself and, therefore, has little or no contractual interface with industry. They are also minimal in Agriculture programs since that agency contracts almost all its extramural research and development with educational and nonprofit institutions. In addition, the firms that do participate in its programs do relatively little research and development on their own and tend to be less patent conscious than those participating in defense/aerospace work.

The direct effect of policy on NSF and HEW programs also appears to be small because most of their contract research is either basic in nature, offering limited opportunities to develop patentable inventions, or is performed by nonprofit institutions who, for the most part, are interested in the research for itself. However, some problems may be encountered in instances of joint or overlapping research at nonprofit institutions where the rights of other parties may be involved. And, a significant indirect effect has been noted in an important HEW health program where voluntary noncontractual participation by a patent sensitive industry was curtailed because of patent considerations.

The Department of Interior, like HEW and NSF, has a number of programs—such as water desalination— which are oriented toward developing basic technologies. The Agency contracts in these areas with research-oriented industrial firms (many of whom are patent conscious), as well as educational and nonprofit institutions, and acquires title to patents arising under its programs. Under some programs, statutes on which they are based have been interpreted to require the agency to acquire rights in existing patents owned by contractors because of their relevance to the contract effort and future utilization of contract results. These factors—patent conscious organizations and acquisition of rights to contract inventions and existing patents—have resulted in several instances of hesitation or refusal to participate in the government program. Insufficient data was available to establish how widespread the reaction was or its overall effect on Interior programs.

The largest number of opportunities for participation problems occur, of course, in DOD, NASA, and AEC programs because of the size and scope of their contract effort. Only a limited amount of data was available on this question for these agencies but a few general observations may be made. At least as to the majority of DOD inventions, to which contractors are normally permitted to retain title, no problem arises. In addition, NASA's policy of waiving title to inventions to promote utilization under appropriate circumstances provides a method for resolving competing government and industry objectives with regard to patents arising under contract. Lastly, interviews with industrial firms in the survey sample indicate that—except where a large investment in private research, know-how, inventions and/or patents considered to be valuable in commercial markets exist—acquisition or improvement of technical skills is sufficiently important to them in most cases to justify participating in government programs in their areas of interest even though patent provisions are not completely suitable to them.

However, this does not mean that either a title or license policy will equally serve the government's interests under all the above circumstances, since the policy selected may also affect industrial decisions to use contract inventions commercially. Here again, a balancing of government objectives appears necessary to ensure that the net effect of the patent policy promotes the government's overall goals.

PART I. The Study Task

The goal of the Harbridge House study has been to determine the effects of government patent policy on the objectives it is designed to achieve. Essentially, these objectives are three:

    (i) Encourage participation in government research and development programs;

    (ii) Promote commercial utilization of government-sponsored inventions; and

    (iii) Foster business competition.

While it is easy to agree on the policy objectives, it is hard to agree on how best to achieve them. Lack of information on the economic effects of the policy has been a major obstacle in this respect. There have been no ready answers to such questions as:

    (i) Is commercial utilization of government inventions achieved best under government or contractor ownership?

    (ii) Is substantial investment over and above that supplied by the government necessary to achieve utilization: If yes, are exclusive rights necessary or useful in attracting private capital for further development, or will such investment be made when everyone is free to use the invention?

    (iii) Do competent firms refuse to undertake government R&D work because of government patent policy? Does the policy affect application of the contractor's most advanced privately developed technology to government projects? Does it affect assignments óf personnel to government contracts? And, does it affect the flow of information between the contractor's government and privately sponsored work?

    (iv) What are the effects on competition of the acquisition of exclusive commercial rights to government-sponsored inventions? Do they increase or decrease concentration in commercial industries; cement or dilute positions of leadership in industry; create or eliminate significant areas of market power?

A major objective of the study has been to acquire and analyze information which would help answer these questions. As described in the Summary and Analysis of Findings the study was accomplished in three phases and the data were gathered through several related tasks, which were researched for 18 months within government, industry, and educational and nonprofit institutions. Since the research data are a significant source of new information on the role of patents within government, industry, and nonprofit institutions, they are reported in some detail in the research reports which comprise Volumes II, III, and IV of the final report. Names of organizations and other information received in confidence are disguised throughout the study.

PART II. The Policy Criteria and the Sources
of Government Invention

The President's statement of policy[1] establishes several criteria for allocating patent rights between the government and its contractors. The criteria tend to align with the R&D programs of specific agencies, resulting in relationships among R&D programs, inventive output and patent rights which help explain the economic effects of government patent policy.

Section 1(a) of the policy provides for the government to retain principal rights when:

(i) The end item is intended for commercial use by the general public or government regulations will require it for public use [Section 1 (a)(1)].

(ii) The principal purpose of the contract is to explore fields concerned with public health or welfare [Section 1(a)(2)].

(iii) The contract pertains to new fields of science and technology in which the government has been the sole or principal developer, and the acquisition of title by a contractor might give him a dominant or preferred commercial position [Section 1(a)(3)].

(iv) The contract requires the operation of a government research or production facility or the coordination and direction of the work of others [Section 1(a)(4)].

Section 1(b) provides for principal rights to the contractor when the purpose of the contract is to "build upon existing knowledge or technology" to develop end items for use by the government, and "the contractor has technical competence directly related to an area in which he has an established nongovernmental commercial position." The party that does not receive principal rights normally receives a royalty-free license to use the invention.

Table 1 relates the policy criteria to the agencies whose programs broadly match them. The agencies are grouped into three categories, depending on the main objectives of their programs: (i) public-service agencies, who conduct R&D programs to benefit the public directly; (ii) mission-oriented agencies, who conduct R&D programs for the agencies' own internal use; and (iii) agencies with mixed activities, who conduct both public-service and internally oriented R&D programs.

The contracts of the public-service agencies (like Agriculture, Interior and HEW) if not governed by statute fall largely under Section 1(a)(1) and 1(a)(2) with title in the government, because of their civilian-orientation.

The contracts of DOD, a mission-oriented agency, are interpreted to fall largely within Section 1(b), with title in the contractor because they are not civilian-oriented and they draw heavily on the existing technical competence of industry. To a lesser extent they also come within Sections 1(a)(2), (3) and (4) with title in the government when inventions are in fields concerned with public health or welfare, DOD is the sole or principal developer in the field, or the contractor operates a government facility or directs the work of others. Lastly, the inventions of agencies with mixed activities (such as FAA, AEC, and NASA) may fall under any criteria depending on the purpose of the specific project and the circumstances under which the invention is made.[2] Generally, inventions arising out of public service activities—such as AEC's research on power sources for an artificial heart—would fall within Sections 1(a)(1) and (2). And, inventions from mission activities would come within one of the other three criteria.

Structural differences within the research and development program have a major effect on the number of inventions produced under the various policy criteria. Patents arising out of government contracts are heavily concentrated in the mission-oriented and mixed-activity agencies. There are several reasons for this. Since they perform most of the R&D contracting—91.1 percent in fiscal 1965 (see Table 1)—these agencies provide a far greater number of opportunities for inventions than public-service agencies. In addition, they contract predominantly with profit-making organizations[3]—over 87 percent in fiscal 1965 (see Table 2)—who attach greater importance to patents than educational and nonprofit institutions, the other major participants in federal R&D programs. And a great portion of their funds are spent in applied research and development, which is a greater source of patentable inventions than tasks in basic research.

---

[1] The President's Memorandum and Statement of Government Patent Policy is set forth in full in Appendix A.

[2] Here again, statutory patent policies exist and govern NASA and AEC. Both those agencies are matched with the President's Policy to evaluate its probable effect on them.

[3] Industrial firms and educational and nonprofit institutions as sources of government-sponsored inventions are described in detail in Volume IV, Part I. The importance of patents and government-sponsored inventions to these organizations and their utilization of them are discussed at length in Volume IV, Parts II, III, and IV.

TABLE 1

CONCENTRATION OF R&D FUNDS (1965) IN RELATION TO AGENCY AND
GOVERNING POLICY CRITERIA AND PATENTS ISSUED (1957, 1962, 1965)
($ in Millions)

Policy Criteria	Agencies	R&D Obligations FY 1965 ($ in Millions)		Patents Issued: Contract Work					
		Extramural	Intramural	1957 Title	1957 License	1962 Title	1962 License	1965 Title	1965 License
I. Principal Rights in Government									
A. Public Service									
1(a)(1)- End item intended for commercial use by general public.	Agriculture	$ 61.7	$155.7	0	0	1	1	2	0
	Interior	38.5	84.4	1	0	1	0	0	0
	HEW	682.7	174.8	2	1	4	2	3	0
	VA	.8	36.9	0	0	0	0	1	0
	TVA	.3	5.5	0	0	0	0	0	0
1(a)(2)- Purpose of contract to explore fields concerned with public health or welfare.	NSF	183.2	14.5	0	0	0	0	0	1
		$967.2 (9%)	$471.8 (16%)	3	1	6	3	6	1
B. Public Service and Mission-Oriented									
1(a)(3)- Contract pertains to new fields with Government as sole or principal developer.	Commerce	$ 19.4	48.5	8	2	7	0	0	0
	FAA	41.7	34.5	0	0	0	8	1	2
1(a)(4)- Contract requires operation of Government research or production facility or coordination and direction of work of others. [1(a)(1), (2) and 1(b) also applicable]	NASA	3,999.9	871.0		4	4	7	19	4
	AEC	1,233.6	32.8	266	33*	289	98*	250	65*
		$5,294.6 (48%)	$986.8 (33%)	274	39	300	113	270	71
II. Principal Rights in Contractor									
1(b)- Contract builds upon existing knowledge and contractor has technical competence and established nongovernmental commercial position. [1(a)(2), (3) and (4) also applicable]	DOD	$4,805.6 (43%)	$1,542.9 (51%)	206	958	221	1,501	407	NA

* AEC rights in these inventions vary. In some it holds a nonexclusive license only. In others it holds a general license with exclusive rights in field of atomic energy.

Source: Annual Report on Government Patent Policy, Federal Council for Science and Technology, June 1966, and study data.

TABLE 2
ALLOCATIONS OF DOMESTIC R&D OBLIGATIONS AMONG
PROFIT - MAKING, EDUCATIONAL, AND NONPROFIT ORGANIZATIONS FOR
FY 1965
($ in Millions)

R&D Obligations	A. Public-Service Agencies								B. Public-Service and Mission-Oriented				C. Mission-Oriented
	Agric.	Interior	Commerce	HEW	VA	TVA	NSF	Total (Percent)	FAA	AEC	NASA	Total (Percent)	DOD
1. Profit-Making Organizations	2.2	13.5	13.3	27.1	.2	0.	27.4	83.7 (8.5)	39.4	743.3	3766.2	4548.9 (86.0)	4274.5 (89.0)
2. Educational Institutions	57.2	10.7	4.3	475.7	.4	.3	130.9	679.5 (68.9)	.8	402.9	208.4	612.1 (11.9)	326.9 (6.8)
3. Other Nonprofit Organizations	2.3	2.4	1.8	153.5	.2	0.	24.8	185.0 (18.8)	1.5	87.2	17.4	106.1 (2.0)	203.9 (4.2)
4. Other	0.	11.9	0.	26.4	0.	0.	.1	38.4 (3.8)	0.	.2	7.9	8.1 (0.1)	.3 (0.)
TOTAL	61.7	38.5	19.4	682.7	.8	.3	183.2	986.6 (100)	41.7	1233.6	3999.9	5275.2 (100)	4805.6 (100)

Public-service agencies, on the other hand, have had few patents from R&D contracts (see Table 1) because their contract programs are small, more oriented toward basic research, and conducted predominantly with educational and nonprofit institutions. In fiscal 1965, they obligated $986.6 million for extramural work, or 8.9 percent of the total obligated for work outside of government agencies (see Table 1), and $864 million— 87.7 percent (see Table 2)—was spent with educational and nonprofit institutions. Specific agencies exceeded that mark, with over 99 percent of Agriculture's, all of TVA's, and more than 92 percent of HEW's share obligated with those institutions.

The net result of these operational patterns is that the Section 1(a) "government title" criteria will apply to very few government-sponsored inventions, while the Section 1(b) "government license" criteria will apply to the great majority. The contract inventions of the mission-oriented and mixed-activity agencies come largely from applied research in the industrial sector, while those of public-service agencies come from basic research at educational and nonprofit institutions. And the great majority of government-sponsored contract inventions come from military-oriented programs of the Department of Defense which bear little relation to consumer uses.

PART III. Effect of Patent Policy
on Commercial Utilization

A. The Utilization Survey

The effect of patent policy on commercial utilization was studied through a survey of government-sponsored inventions reported in Volume IV.[1] The histories of some 2,100 inventions were examined to determine the role of patent policy in their use.[2]

In addition, other factors that affect utilization—such as prior experience, size of firm, mix of government and commercial work, government promotion of inventions, and amount of private investment required to ready inventions for market—were analyzed to estimate the importance of government patent policy as a business incentive.

Interviews and case studies were conducted of contractors and licensees, the two major users of government-sponsored inventions, to determine the reasons for basic differences in their patterns of utilization: except for two inventions, utilization with title occurred entirely among contractors of the Department of Defense, while utilization under license occurred almost entirely

---

[1] Invention utilization questionnaires were sent to contractors who made government-sponsored inventions patented in 1957 and 1962, and for agencies other than DOD and AEC—patented from 1956 to 1966. Questionnaires were also sent to organizations that received licenses of government-owned inventions they did not develop. These inventions included a group developed by government employees. NASA inventions were not included in the survey to avoid duplicating a recent report on that agency, but the findings of that report have been considered in preparing this study.

[2] When the questionnaire responses had been analyzed (see Volume IV, Part I), four additional tasks were performed to complete the information on the sample:
(i) A group of invention utilizers, deemed high and low (which rationale is set forth in Part II of Volume IV, with the results of the task), were interviewed to determine what business factors have the greatest effect on utilization.
(ii) The inventions of three public-service oriented agencies—Agriculture, Interior, and TVA—were researched to determine what effect agency mission has on utilization. The results of this task are reported in Part III of Volume IV.
(iii) A representative group of educational nonprofit institutions were interviewed to determine what role they play in utilization. The results of this task are reported in Part IV of Volume IV.
(iv) All firms reporting refusals to license sample inventions were interviewed and all inventions involved in infringement suits were investigated to determine the effect of patent policy on business competition. The results of this task are reported in Part V of Volume IV.
Responses were received on about 65 percent of the approximately 4,000 questionnaires sent to organization in the utilization survey.

---

among licensees of the AEC and the public-service agencies.

The role of educational and nonprofit institutions in utilization was a third aspect of the survey. Inventors of more than 10 percent of the inventions studied, these institutions participate in the R&D programs of almost all government agencies. While they do not use these inventions directly because their activities are essentially noncommercial, they do license them for use by others. The survey was concerned with the effect of their licensing activities on utilization.[3] Findings on these three groups of users are summarized below and reported at length in Volume IV, Parts II, III, and IV.

B. Extent of Commercial Utilization

The survey showed that commercial utilization of government-sponsored inventions is very low. Contractors and licensees reported only 251, or 12.4 percent, of all inventions in the survey response in use. Only 55, or 2.7 percent, played a critical role in the commercial products in which they were used, as compared to utilization rates of 50 percent or more estimated for inventions developed under private research. Measured in sales, utilization amounted to $616 million through 1966—$406 million of which was attributable to contractors and $210 million to licensees.

1. Contractor Sales and Development Costs

Table 3 shows the sales and private development costs associated with the 200 inventions used by contractors. Of the 200, DOD sponsored 198, to credit it with the major impact on utilization. Of the $406 million in sales, all but $271,000 are also attributable to DOD inventions.

Sales of critically important contractor inventions are a little over half the total—$193.6 million from domestic sales and $47.3 million from sales abroad; $241 million in all.[4] *Five inventions,* accounting for approximately *88 percent* of the sales in the group, involve the following technologies: *transistors, vacuum tubes, numerical control devices, computers, and gas turbine engines.* The remaining 44 critically important contractor inventions

---

[3] This task is reported in full in Volume IV, Part IV.

[4] In grouping the data, sales involving critically important inventions (those which were clearly responsible for commercial sales) were separated from those involving supporting inventions which played an incidental role in sales of commercial products.

TABLE 3
SALES AND DEVELOPMENT COSTS ASSOCIATED WITH COMMERCIAL
UTILIZATION OF INVENTIONS BY CONTRACTORS (1957 AND 1962)
($ in millions)

	Amount[1] of Actual Domestic Sales From:		Amount[1] of Actual Foreign Sales From:		Development Costs:				Number of Licenses in Use for Inventions With:	
	Critically Important Inventions	Inventions With a Supporting Role	Critically Important Inventions	Inventions With a Supporting Role	Amount[1] ($)	Average[2] Percent in Technical Development	Average[2] Percent in Production Facilities	Average[2] Percent in Marketing	Critical Role	Supporting Role
Total Sample	193.63	117.07	47.28	47.65	26.33	56.8	22.7	20.5	31	40
DOD	193.48	117.05	47.18	47.65	25.88	56.8	21.9	21.3	29	38
AEC	0	.021	0	0	.201	52.5	45	2.5	1	2
Other Agencies	.15	0	.10	0	.25	70	20	10	1	0
1957 DOD	100.85	103.37	45.80	40.32	3.59	58.3	20	21.7	12	13
1962 DOD	92.63	13.68	1.38	7.33	22.29	56.2	22.7	21.1	17	25

[1] To date of response to questionnaire.
[2] Average for those responding to this question only.

totaled only $29 million in sales. This amounts to annual[5] sales of $20 million for the five inventions with high sales and about $659,090 for the other inventions in that class.

In relating sales to the concentration of patent holdings, it was found that not one of the top ten patent owners has a sample invention with cumulative sales of more than $2 million, even though the group holds 52 percent of all the patents. Only one firm, ranked in the 11 to 25 group, had a patent with significant utilization—$70 million to the date of the survey.

When private development costs were compared with utilization, it was found that firms spent at least $26 million in bringing the inventions into commercial use. It is difficult to generalize on these data because many firms provided no information. However, the data available does indicate that about 56 percent of private funds were spent in technical development and the balance was divided about equally between production facilities and marketing.

2. **Licensee Sales and Development Costs**

Table 4 shows comparable sales and development costs associated with licensed government-owned inventions. The government issued 342 licenses on 126 survey inventions, ten of which were used by 50 licensees.[6] These inventions are concentrated in agencies other than the Department of Defense.[7] The AEC and the Department of Agriculture account for the largest number, owning 65 percent of these patents and issuing 55 percent of the licenses.

Domestic and foreign sales to the date of the survey were $210.3 million, compared to $405 million for contractor inventions. All but $7.03 million of this is attributable to inventions which play a critical role in their commercial use.

Unlike contractor inventions where sales related primarily to DOD inventions, DOD-related sales here account for only .4 percent ($75,000) of the total.

[5] Computed from the date of patent application to the date of the survey. Three years were allowed for filing an application prior to issuance of patent. On this basis, the availability of 1957 inventions is 13 years; and of 1962 inventions, eight years. The average availability is 10.5 years for inventions in both sample years.

[6] Since it is common knowledge that government-owned inventions may be used without a formal license, it is probable that more inventions are being used than are noted in government records, although no data were available as to the exact number.
[7] DOD owns only 19 percent of the inventions and issued only 9 percent of the licenses.

TABLE 4
SALES AND PRIVATE DEVELOPMENT COSTS ASSOCIATED WITH COMMERCIAL
UTILIZATION OF GOVERNMENT-OWNED PATENTS BY NON-INVENTOR LICENSEES
($ in millions)

	Amount[1] of Actual Domestic Sales From:		Amount[1] of Actual Foreign Sales From:		Development Costs[2]			
	Critically Important Inventions	Inventions with a Supporting Role	Critically Important Inventions	Inventions with a Supporting Role	Amount[1]	Average Percent in Technical Development	Average Percent in Production Facilities	Average Percent in Marketing
Total Sample	201.12	6.945	2.2	.085	5.389	21.1	52.2	26.7
DOD	.02	.055	0	0	.040	70	30	0
AEC	.40	0	0	0	.020	50	25	25
Agriculture	196.5	.025	2.2	.085	3.118	17.1	47.9	35
TVA	4.20	5.34	0	0	2.211	16.9	58.9	24.2
Other Agencies	0	1.525	0	0	0	0	0	0

[1] To date of response to questionnaire.
[2] Average for those responding to this question only.

Agriculture and TVA are the largest contributors of commercial inventions, and, here again, the extreme variability in commercial potential of government patents, seen first in connection with contractor inventions, is evident. Three patents involved in the manufacture of potato flakes account for about half the sales from Agriculture inventions.

As with contractor inventions, reports on private development costs were sketchy. Licensees reported $5.389 million in development expense, with a much smaller share—21.1 percent—going toward technical development of the invention and a much larger share—52.2 percent—going toward production facilities than was the case with contractor inventions. The shift in emphasis, we believe, is because the public service agencies sponsor inventions with greater commercial orientation and, in addition, carry development of their inventions further toward a commercially useful form. Table 4 shows the high percentage of costs going to technical development for DOD and AEC inventions (matching the pattern of contractor inventions in Table 3) as compared to the costs for Agriculture and TVA patents.

3. Utilization of Inventions from the Institutional Environment

Commercialization of institutional patents is increasingly contemplated by private and public institutions of higher education, in need of funds as educational costs outrun traditional sources of revenue. Patent activity in nonprofit research corporations has also been increasing, as a means of financing independent research and development programs.

The rise of interest in patents among nonprofit institutions has been fanned by reports in the press and popular periodicals about the "gold mine" of patentable research findings. Scarcely a month goes by without a report or a feature article on a cigarette filter and Columbia University, ammoniated dentifrice at Indiana University, Wisconsin's vitamins, or a super-juice called "Gator Ade" at the University of Florida. These reports are invariably sprinkled with seven-digit royalty income figures—$14 million from Vitamin D at Wisconsin, $7 million from streptomycin at Rutgers, and so on. Finally, there are allusions to the profit potential in the ocean outside of the Scripps Institute of Oceanography, in the sky above the California Institute of Technology, and in the black boxes of M.I.T.

The facts, however, do not support the thesis that the average nonprofit research organization can expect to realize any substantial income from patent royalties. The liberal arts college in Volume IV, Part IV, Case 10, which has enjoyed an unexpected and large return on a pre-World War II invention, acknowledges it as a windfall and deemphasizes patents accordingly. The technical institution in Volume IV, Part IV, Case 5, one of the five organizations interviewed that actually receives annual royalty income of six figures, still regards patent administration as marginal from a purely financial point of view. The average net annual royalty income of the three institutions of higher learning with the most active programs in the study was $100,000. Several institutions were currently enjoying higher incomes attributable to a single invention or the settlement of a law suit, but in no case did royalty income approach that of an industrial scale.

As reported by *The Patent, Trademark and Copyright Journal*,[8] the average annual gain for each utilized patent is about $70,000. This figure seems high to us, since our study revealed that firms frequently overstate the value of a patent by equating revenue accruing from the invention with end-product sales. In addition, the figure of $70,000 does not resemble the return on inventions to nonprofit institutions.

Overall, only 10 percent of the survey inventions from nonprofit institutions reached commercial utilization. One of the patent development firms interviewed in our study estimates that 10 to 15 percent of the disclosures it receives result in patents three to four years after submission; 25 percent of these patents are eventually licensed, with 3 percent profitable. As for dollar value, once every three years a university invention is likely to result in an annual royalty of $50,000 or more.

Expectation of large returns, which appears to be a principal motivation behind the upsurge in patent interest among nonprofit organizations, is not likely to be fulfilled for many of them. At best, a well-organized patent program, using the personnel required to meet reporting commitments under government contracts, may expect to reap a modest return for a nonprofit organization.

C. Concentration of Patent Holdings and Utilizations

1. Contractor-Owned Inventions

Both utilization and patent holdings of survey inventions are heavily concentrated in a few firms. Table 5 shows the levels of concentration among the top 50 responders. Consistent with the concentration of R&D funds in industry generally, the top five hold rights in 31.2 percent of the inventions and account for 27.2 percent of the inventions utilized. The top 25 hold 70.7 percent of the inventions and 67.6 percent of the utilizations.

---

[8] "The Economic Impact of Patents," 2: 340-362, 1958.

Concentration slows markedly with the next 25 firms, the top 50 holding rights in 82.9 percent of the inventions and achieving 81 percent of the utilizations. Although the overall rate of utilization is 10.4 percent, the record of the top 50 firms is consistently below that mark. Only 65 of 192 responders reported any commercial utilization at all.

2. Invention Holdings and Utilization by Firm and Percent Government Business

Table 6A shows the percent distribution of holdings and utilization of sample patents by size of firm and percent government business. Both patent rights and utilization of inventions are heavily concentrated in large companies. Firms with annual sales over $200 million account for about 37 percent of the responders but hold rights (title and license) in 80 percent of the inventions and account for 72 percent of the utilization. Table 6A indicates that these same firms (annual sales over $200 million) have the following characteristics:

   (i) Firms in the 0 to 20 percent government business category include 20 percent of the responders, have title in 33.9 percent of the inventions, and account for 19 percent of the inventions utilized;

  (ii) Firms in the 20 to 50 percent government business category comprise 5 percent of the responders, have title in 19.8 percent of the inventions, and account for 27.5 percent of the inventions utilized;

 (iii) Firms in the 50 to 80 percent category include 2.5 percent of the responders, have title in 8.4 percent of the inventions, and account for 12.5 percent of the inventions utilized; and

  (iv) Firms in the 80 to 100 percent government business category make up 8 percent of the responders, have title in 17.6 percent of the inventions, and account for 13.5 percent of the inventions utilized.

Highlighting the record of this group of firms with sales over $200 million is the heavy concentration—20 percent of all responders—of firms doing 20 percent or less of their business with the government. These firms own a larger share of inventions (33.9 percent) than they have utilized (19 percent). In contrast, large firms in the 20 to 50 percent category constitute a much smaller percentage of the responders (5 percent) but proportionately own (19.8 percent) and use (27.5 percent) many more inventions than any other class of firms in the sample. Large firms doing 80 to 100 percent of their business with the government comprised only 8 percent of the responders, but they owned (17.6 percent) and

TABLE 5
CONCENTRATION OF CONTRACTOR PATENT HOLDINGS IN THE SAMPLE, RESPONSE RATE, AND
RATE OF COMMERCIAL UTILIZATION: ALL AGENCIES BOTH SAMPLE YEARS[1]

Number of Firms	Number of Patents in			Percent[5] of Total Patents in			% Average Utilization Percent[6]
	Sample[2]	Response[3]	C. U. [4]	Sample	Response	C. U.	
Top Five[7]	721	662	57	31.2	32.6	27.2	8.6
10	1,150	1,047	92	49.7	51.6	43.8	8.8
25	1,635	1,479	142	70.7	73.0	67.6	9.6
50	1,919	1,735	170	82.9	85.6	81.0	9.8
Total	2,316	2,024	210	100.0	100.0	100.0	10.4
In Sample, No Response	1,082						

Number of Firms:
(1) Responding 192
(2) Not Responding 271
(3) Total 463
(4) With At Least One C.U. 65

[1] Total sample includes all patents developed by contractors and issued in 1957 and 1962, except those developed under NASA contracts and 415 AEC inventions.
[2] "Sample" means the total population of patents as defined in footnote 1.
[3] "Response" indicates the number of patents for which questionnaires were returned.
[4] "C. U." indicates that commercial utilization has been achieved for this patent, by the inventing contractor.
[5] Percent in each case is the percent of the total patents of responding firms in the sample, the response, and in commercial utilization. For example, a total of 210 patents in C. U. and the top five firms held 57 or 27.2 percent of these patents in C. U.
[6] Calculated by taking the sum of patents in C. U. over the sum of patents in the response for each size class.
[7] Ranking is by order of number of questionnaires in the response.

used (13.5 percent) a larger share of inventions than their share of responses.

Grouping firms by percent government business rather than by size, Table 6A shows that firms with 20 percent or less in government work have the most patent activity but not the most utilizations. Comprising 43.5 percent of the responders, this group owns 38.9 percent of the inventions and accounts for 29.0 percent of the utilization. Firms in the 80 to 100 percent category are second in level of activity, comprising 31.5 percent of the responders, 26.4 percent of the titles, and 21 percent of the utilization. Firms in the 20 to 50 category, however, show a better record of utilization than any other group. Constituting 23.6 percent of the inventions, they account for 32 percent of the utilization. The high utilization is due primarily to the large firms (over $200 million) in the group. Firms in the 50 to 80 percent category show fairly low levels of activity; comprising 11 percent of the responders, they own 12 percent of the patents and account for 18 percent of the utilization.

3. Government-Owned Inventions

Concentration of license holdings and utilization of government-owned inventions presents a very different picture from contractor inventions. As Table 6B shows, holdings and utilization are very heavily concentrated in small firms with less than $5 million in sales who do 20 percent or less of their business with the government. These firms account for 68 percent of the utilization of government-owned patents. Large firms with over $200 million in sales utilized almost no inventions they did not develop except for a small segment doing 20 percent or less of their business with the government. Thus the pattern of holdings and utilization is exactly the reverse of the pattern for contractor inventions.

Significantly, utilization of licenses is concentrated among inventions developed by TVA and Agriculture, as shown in Table 7. These agencies account for 45 of the 50 users among licensees and six of the 10 utilized inventions. The R&D programs of these agencies are

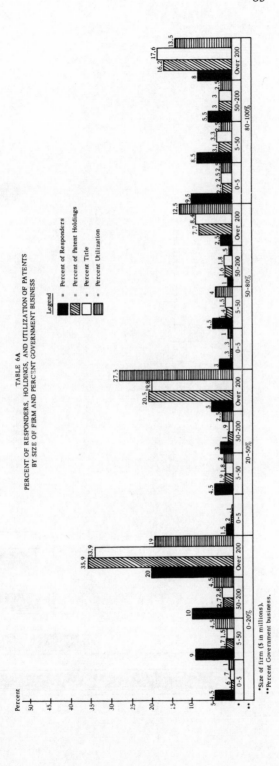

TABLE 6A
PERCENT OF RESPONDERS, HOLDINGS, AND UTILIZATION OF PATENTS
BY SIZE OF FIRM AND PERCENT GOVERNMENT BUSINESS

Legend

■ = Percent of Responders
▨ = Percent of Patent Holdings
☐ = Percent Title
▥ = Percent Utilization

*Size of firm ($ in millions).
**Percent Government business.

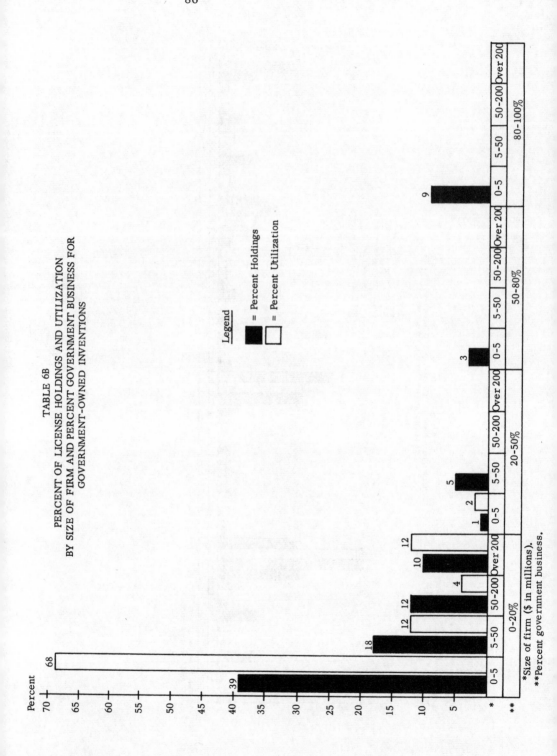

TABLE 6B

PERCENT OF LICENSE HOLDINGS AND UTILIZATION
BY SIZE OF FIRM AND PERCENT GOVERNMENT BUSINESS FOR
GOVERNMENT-OWNED INVENTIONS

Legend

■ = Percent Holdings
□ = Percent Utilization

*Size of firm ($ in millions).
**Percent government business.

TABLE 7.–
NUMBER OF USES PER GOVERNMENT-OWNED INVENTION

	Total	DOD	AEC	TVA	Agriculture	Other
Inventions in Use	10	2	1	2	4	1
Number of Users	50	2	2	36	9	1
Number of Inventions Used						
Most Frequent Use	1 @ 32			1 @ 32		
Second Most Frequent Use	1 @ 3				1 @ 3	
Third Most Frequent Use	1 @ 2		1 @ 2			
Once	7 @ 1	2 @ 1		1 @ 1	3 @ 1	1 @ 1
Number Not Specified By Invention	6			3	3	

heavily oriented to civilian needs, and they normally develop their inventions fully for consumer use and actively promote utilization by manufacturers and the ultimate consumer.[9] This combination of factors is largely responsible for their high record of utilization while retaining title.

D. Factors Affecting Utilization

1. Contractor-Owned Inventions

With the patterns of patent activity in the survey identified, the data were analyzed as to the major factors affecting utilization. Contractor rights, prior experience, percent government business, size of firm, field of technology, form of invention, kind of agency, and year of patents were all tested for their effect on commercial use.

a. *Patent Rights, Prior Experience, and Year of Patent.* Of all the factors, patent rights and prior experience show the strongest association with commercial utilization. Table 8 correlates these factors and the year of patent with the rate of utilization. The year of the patent issue appears to have little effect on utilization, but utilization drops from 23.8 to 13.3 percent when exclusive rights are not available[10] and from 23.8 to 6.6 percent when prior experience is not present.

---

[9] Volume III describes the promotional programs of Agriculture, TVA, and six other agencies.

[10] It is not possible to state categorically that exclusive rights in themselves are responsible for the shift in utilization since contractors had the option to acquire or waive title to most of these inventions under DOD contracts, and presumably waived title only when the invention clearly was of no use to them.

TABLE 8
CORRELATION OF PATENT RIGHTS, PRIOR EXPERIENCE, YEAR OF PATENT, AND COMMERCIAL UTILIZATION

Characteristics of Invention	Rate of Commercial Utilization (percent[1])	Observations (No. Utilized/ Total No. Observations)
Year of Patent		
1. 1962 patent, contractor has title and prior experience	22.8	78/341
2. 1957 patent, contractor has title and prior experience	25.6	50/195
Title (both years)		
1. Contractor has title and prior experience	23.8	128/536
2. Contractor has no title, but has prior experience	13.3	8/60
Prior Experience (both years)		
1. Contractor has prior experience, but no title	13.3	8/60
2. Contractor has no prior experience, but has title	6.6	63/948
3. Contractor has no prior experience and no title	2.2	4/176

[1] Computed by dividing the number utilized by the total number of observations.

Significantly, prior experience has an even greater effect on utilization than does ownership of the patent, as the case studies in Volume IV, part II confirm. Interviews of 10 high and 11 low utilizers showed that, in most large firms, the decision to use a government invention is quite separate from the decision to patent. Most frequently the decision to patent is based on a desire to ensure freedom of design, to protect against infringement suits, to cross license, to recognize employee inventiveness, or to enhance the firm's image. In most instances, utilization counts only as a speculation that the invention may have some commercial use. Tables 9 and 10 provide some measure of the weight given the commercial value of government inventions by these firms. With the exception of three companies who do most of their business with the government, all file one-third or less of their patent applications on government-sponsored inventions.

b. *Field of Technology, Size of Firm, and Percent Government Business.* Three other factors—the field of technology, the size of the firm, and the percent government business—were found to affect the rate of commercial utilization statistically.

Table 11 shows that mechanical inventions have a higher rate of utilization than inventions in other fields of technology. Prior experience again strongly influences utilization, but apparently less for mechanical inventions than for those in other fields of technology.

The combined effect on utilization[11] of size of firm and percent government business is shown in Figure I-1. As we have already discussed, large firms in government markets tend to patent for reasons more than planned use of the invention, resulting in their lower rates of utilizations as shown in Figure I-1. Case studies show that some firms who do most of their work for the government do not try to apply the inventions commercially and, therefore, have low rates of utilization. Smaller firms and those more oriented to commercial markets achieve higher utilization because they patent more selectively and have the necessary experience to develop market innovations in their product lines.

Even for firms with the highest rates of utilization, however, the amount of utilization is very small when measured in sales. Thus, the factors affecting utilization, described above, affect it only within a narrow range of performance. The most basic factor, as noted in Volume IV, Part II, is the commercial potential of the sample

---

[11] The rate of commercial utilization is computed differently in Figure I-1 than in the Table 6 above. Utilization percentages in Table 6 represent a group's share in all inventions used. Utilization rates in Figure I-1 represent the percent of a group's holdings that it has been able to utilize.

inventions and all other factors make a difference only when inventions reach a minimum threshold of commercial utility. Not many of the inventions involved in the study have reached that point.

c. *Industry Attitudes Toward Patents on Government-Sponsored Inventions.*

(1) *Introduction.* Industry's attitudes toward patents on government-sponsored inventions are an important factor in utilization even though these attitudes cannot be evaluated statistically. The 21 high and low utilizers of contractor inventions interviewed in the survey were found to have six dominant attitudes toward patents, which condition their reaction to government patent policy and govern their actions in participating in, and using the inventions of, government programs. Firms were classed as high utilizers if they used more than 12 percent of their inventions commercially and as low utilizers if they utilized less than 7 percent.

Figure I-2 categorizes the 21 companies according to dominant attitudes, size distribution, and industry. As shown in Tables 12 and 13, these firms account for 53.7 percent of the survey inventions, 131 of the 210 utilized inventions, and, at least, $179 million of the $406 million in sales reported for contractor inventions.

(2) *Patents Have No Importance.* A lack of interest in patents was characteristic of some research-oriented and manufacturing firms that do either a preponderance or a large percentage of their business in the government aerospace and defense markets. Three such firms—Companies A, F, and K, ranging in size from the $5 to $50 million category to over $200 million in annual sales (see Figure I-2)—indicated no desire to expand into commercial markets and no mechanism for the commercialization of inventions. These three firms account for only 1.8 percent of the inventions of the companies interviewed. Although Company A is shown as a high utilizer in Table 12, its attitude toward patents has changed since the early sixties, and it no longer pursues commercial utilization of inventions developed by its government divisions. When these firms (A, K, and F) obtain patents under government contracts, their sole purpose is recognition of technical competence within the company.

(3) *Patents Are of Little Value, Compared with Technical Know-How.* Firms expressing this attitude toward patents generally are manufacturers of such complex systems and technical products as aircraft, jet engines, computers, or communications equipment. Although as much as 75 percent of their sales may be

TABLE 9
INTERNAL PATENT MANAGEMENT
TEN HIGH UTILIZERS

Company	Size of Firm ($ in millions)	% Government Business	Number of Applications Filed Per Year (Approx.)	% Government-Sponsored Applications*	% Company-Sponsored Applications*
Q	over 1,000	65-80	Not Available	20	80
S	over 1,000	40	960	12	88
A	200 -1,000	40	75	33 1/3	66 2/3
G	200 -1,000	30-40	150	15	85
R	200 -1,000	10	500	10	90
E	50 - 200	85	125	14	86
H	50 - 200	75	75	25-30	70-75
N	50 - 200	70	140	25	75
M	5 - 50	10-40	25-30	25	75
J	under 5	20-50	Not Available	Not Available	Not Available

*Percentages are approximate.

TABLE 10
INTERNAL PATENT MANAGEMENT
ELEVEN LOW UTILIZERS

Company	Size of Firm ($ in millions)	% Government Business	Number of Applications Filed Per Year (Approx.)	% Government-Sponsored Applications*	% Company-Sponsored Applications*
B	over 1,000	80	1,000-2,000	2-5	95-98
C	over 1,000	2	510	1 (-)	99+
I	over 1,000	75	300- 350	33 1/3	66 2/3
O	over 1,000	50-90	70	25	75
P	over 1,000	95	175- 200	50	50
T	over 1,000	30	600	10-15	85-90
D	200- 1,000	10	1,000	0 (since 1962)	100 (since 1962)
U	200- 1,000	55-70	250	20	80
F	5- 50	85	Not Available	Not Available	Not Available
K	5- 50	90	5-6	100	0
L	under 5	Not Available	30	65	35

*Percentages are approximate.

TABLE 11
EFFECT OF FIELD OF TECHNOLOGY ON UTILIZATION

	Commercial Use with Title and Prior Experience		Commercial Use with Title but No Prior Experience	
	Percent	Observations	Percent	Observations
Mechanical Inventions	33.3	40/120	11.0	25/227
Inventions in Other Fields of Technology	20.6	89/431	5.2	38/725

FIGURE I - 1
RELATIONSHIP AMONG SIZE OF FIRM, PERCENT GOVERNMENT BUSINESS,
AND THE RATE OF COMMERCIAL UTILIZATION[1]

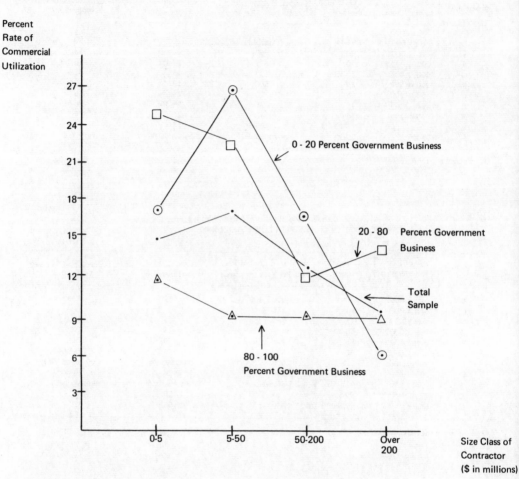

[1] Defined as patents in commercial use/patents in response.

FIGURE 1-2
DOMINANT INDUSTRIAL ATTITUDES TOWARD PATENTS
AMONG TEN HIGH AND ELEVEN LOW UTILIZERS
(CONTRACTOR INVENTIONS)

1. **Patents have no importance**

Company F - $5-50 million * - Industry 4 ** - 85% ***
Company K - $50-200 million - Industry 6   - 90%
Company A - $200 - 1 billion - Industry 3   - 40%

2. **Patents are of little value, compared
with technical know-how**

Company E - $200 M - 1 billion - Industry 4 - 85%
Company B - Over $1 billion   - Industry 5 - 80%
Company O - Over $1 billion   - Industry 1 - 50-90%
Company P - Over $1 billion   - Industry 1 - 95%
Company Q - Over $1 billion   - Industry 2 - 65-80%
Company U - $200 M - 1 billion - Industry 3 - 55-70%
Company R - $200 M - 1 billion - Industry 2 - 10%

3. **Patents are valuable for
defensive purposes**

Company B - Over $1 billion   - Industry 5 - 80%
Company G - $200 M - 1 billion - Industry 5 - 30-40%
Company H - $50 - 200 million - Industry 5 - 75%
Company I - Over $1 billion   - Industry 5 - 75%
Company O - Over $1 billion   - Industry 1 - 50-90%
Company P - Over $1 billion   - Industry 1 - 95%

4. **Patents are important in establishing
proprietary positions**

Company C - Over $1 billion   - Industry 7 - 2%
Company J - Under $5 million - Industry 6 - 20-50%
Company L - Under $5 million - Industry 6 - N/A ****
Company T - Over $1 billion   - Industry 3 - 30%

5. **Patents are essential to
business activities**

Company L - Under $5 million - Industry 6 - N/A ⎫
Company M - $5-50 million   - Industry 7 - 10-40% ⎬ Pattern 1
Company N - $50-200 million - Industry 4 - 70% ⎭

Company C - Over $1 billion   - Industry 7 - 2% ⎫ Pattern 2
Company D - Over $1 billion   - Industry 7 - 10% ⎭

6. **Patents are judged differently in
commercial and government work**

Company C - Over $1 billion - Industry 7 - 2%
Company D - Over $1 billion - Industry 7 - 10%
Company S - Over $1 billion - Industry 3 - 40%

---

* Indicates range of annual sales at time survey patents were issued.

** Industry Key:
   1 Military & Space Systems & Airframe Manufacturers
   2 Aircraft Engines & Components Manufacturers
   3 Diversified Products & Service Firms (military & commercial)
   4 Instruments, Components & Subsystems Manufacturers
   5 Electronic & Communications Equipment Manufacturers
   6 R & D Firms
   7 Commercial Product Firms

*** Indicates approximate percent government business during sample years.

**** Not available

TABLE 12
INVENTION UTILIZATION
TEN HIGH UTILIZERS
(CONTRACTOR INVENTIONS)

| Company | Rank in Patent Holdings[1] | Patent Holdings | | | | Number Utilized | Number Utilized With Commercial Sales Over $1 Million | Total Commercial Sales Million-Dollar Inventions |
		Title	License	Number	% of Sample			
Company S	1	153	21	174	7.8	43	3	3.0
Company R	6	110	0	110	5.4	13	2	7.2
Company Q	10	52	4	56	2.7	13	1	1.0
Company E	14	36	0	36	1.7	5	1	1.0
Company H	20	22	0	22	1.0	7	0	0.0
Company A	22	20	0	20	.9	7	1	2.0
Company G	24	15	4	19	.9	4	2	70.0
Company J	25	18	1	19	.9	3	0	0.0
Company N	31	13	0	13	.6	5	3	22.2
Company M	45	8	0	8	.3	3	1	1.25
TOTAL				477	22.2	103	14	107.65

[1] Rank based on holdings of both title and license to inventions in the survey sample.

directly to the government, these firms frequently sell similar products to commercial markets. Inventions developed during the course of R&D activities tend to be auxiliary components and subsystems or incremental improvements to the basic product, not as important in sustaining sales or selling new products as are the basic engineering management and production capability of the firm. New ideas and inventions are incorporated in product modifications or in new models and little consideration is given to the protection offered by patent rights. Using a new idea to enhance product performance is regarded as more important than assuring that the company owns the exclusive right to use it.

The seven firms with this attitude, three of whom are also listed under the attitude which follows, all have annual sales over $200 million (see Figure I-2). They include three high and four low utilizers, who as a group, hold 22.9 percent of both the survey patents and 36.6 percent of the utilized inventions. More importantly, however, these seven firms are responsible for $81.2 million, or almost half, of the sales of the entire group of high and low utilizers. Just three inventions, however, account for $79.2 million of that, showing again the

"sweepstakes" effect in utilization of government-sponsored inventions.

(4) *Patents are Valuable for Defensive Purposes.* Some firms believe strongly that corporate ownership of patents is important to maintain flexibility in design, both in the United States and abroad (through ownership of corresponding foreign patent rights), and to provide trading material for cross-licenses with competitive firms. Ownership of a patent as a prerequisite for new product development, however, is a relatively minor factor with these firms compared with market and investment considerations associated with commercialization of the invention. Five of the six firms with this attitude are large companies with sales over $200 million. The sixth, Company H, has sales in the $50 to $200 million range (see Figure I-2). The three new firms, (Companies G, H, and I) included here hold about 8 percent of the patents and utilization, including one highly used invention, contributing $70 million in sales to its owner.

A change in government patent policy may affect some firms in this category by causing them to choose

TABLE 13
INVENTION UTILIZATION
ELEVEN LOW UTILIZERS
(CONTRACTOR INVENTIONS)

Company	Rank in Patent Holdings	Patent Holdings				Number Utilized	Number Utilized With Commercial Sales Over $1 Million	Total Commercial Sales Million-Dollar Inventions
		Title	License	Number	% of Sample			
Company I	2	84	47	131	6.5	5	0	0.0
Company B	4	118	1	119	5.8	5	1	22.0
Company T	5	67	50	117	5.7	3	0	0.0
Company P	7	75	7	82	4.0	5	0	0.0
Company C	9	57	5	62	3.0	0	0	0.0
Company U	12	39	3	42	2.0	3	2	50.0
Company O	16	30	0	30	1.4	4	0	0.0
Company L	19	26	0	26	1.2	0	0	0.0
Company D	21	13	9	22	1.0	3	0	0.0
Company F	35	11	0	11	.5	0	0	0.0
Company K	39	8	1	9	.4	0	0	0.0
TOTAL				651	31.5	28	3	72.0

more carefully the areas in which they are willing to undertake government research. Faced with the possibility of being unable to obtain title to patents they develop, these firms may refuse to contract in research areas that would impair their operational flexibility.

(5) *Patents Are Important in Establishing Proprietary Positions.* Firms having this attitude actively seek ownership of patents to establish and maintain proprietary positions in new technologies as well as in established product areas. Invariably, however, estimates of market potential and corporate investment requirements determine which product areas are developed. The makeup of the patent portfolio of these firms may indicate the direction for product development in order to strengthen proprietary positions, but development is rarely, if ever, undertaken solely because patent protection is available.

Of the four firms showing this attitude, two (J and L) are small (less than $5 million sales) and two (C and T) are large (more than $1 billion in sales). One of the small firms is a high utilizer; the other small firm and the two large firms are low utilizers. The large firms hold 8.8

percent of the patents and about 2.3 percent of the utilizations. The small firms hold 2.1 percent of the patents and 1.5 percent of the utilizations. The low record of utilization by the small firms in this group masks their importance as potential commercializers of government inventions. They actively seek new product ideas in the R&D work they perform and, consequently, they have very different outlooks from the firms described under (2) above. That their utilization is low is partially due to the fact that they often participate in advanced R&D government programs where the chances for immediate commercial spillover are small.

A change in government policy from license rights to title rights would limit the government-sponsored R&D activity of firms in this category because of possible conflict with company-sponsored research activities. These companies would examine contract opportunities on an individual basis and, in many cases, might refuse to contract with the government.

(6) *Patents Are Essential to Business Activities.* Firms in this category regard patent rights as essential to their business activities, and are careful to avoid

government claims or conflicts over ownership of inventions. Their policies generally lead them into one of two business patterns. In the first pattern, firms will assure corporate ownership of patents before initiating work on a government contract, either by negotiating contracts that permit them to acquire title to patents on inventions they may develop, or by developing and patenting basic inventions with limited private funds and then seeking contract work in order to develop additional technical competence, push the state of the art, explore a new technology, or determine if commercial applications may begin to be drawn off. In these situations, firms deliberately select areas of government research to match their commercial interests in order to generate product ideas with commercial possibilities. New research firms with strong technical abilities and limited capital typically follow this pattern, as do specialized firms that have concentrated their business in a limited area of technology. The three firms in the first pattern (L, M, and N) are small to medium-sized companies, ranging from less than $5 million in sales to $50 to $200 million. One of these (Company L) is included under (5) above; the other two hold .9 percent of the inventions and account for about 6 percent of the utilizations. Though these holdings are small, one of the two (N) has three inventions which account for $22.2 million, or about 12 percent of the total sales of inventions by high and low utilizers.

In the second pattern, firms isolate government work from their commercial operations and pursue these activities separately. Frequently, inventions derived from government contract work will be assigned automatically to the government to avoid title conflicts or commingling with company-sponsored R&D. In other cases, government R&D will be undertaken only in areas where there is no potential conflict with corporate proprietary objectives and in order to enhance the corporate image. The technical value of government contracts to the commercial interests of these firms is rarely considered a valuable supplement to in-house research and development.

The two firms in the second pattern (C and D) are large firms with more than $1 billion in sales. They hold 4 percent of the inventions and account for 2.2 percent of the utilizations. Those firms following the second business pattern have no proprietary expectations from government contracts. Any change in government patent policy with respect to license and title rights would have little effect on them since they have already divorced their main corporate interest from government contract work and do not regard government-sponsored R&D as a source of commercial ideas.

Firms following the first pattern, however, would be severely affected by a change in policy since their business activity is based largely on government-sponsored research that may develop commercial applications. Corporate ownership of patents is, therefore, an essential feature of the growth strategy of such firms. If title to inventions arising from government-sponsored research were to become unavailable, such firms would have to either change their mode of business or refuse to contract with the government.

(7) *Patents Are Judged Differently in Commercial and Government Work.* Many diversified companies follow different patent policies in their commercial and government markets. These firms may place a strong emphasis on maintaining proprietary positions in commercial markets and express a relative lack of interest in patents arising from government work. It is difficult to generalize about these firms except to note that their policies tend to follow the patterns of the industries in which their divisions participate. Their behavior may, therefore, resemble any of the categories of firms described above if their divisions have similar business profiles.

All three firms in this category (Companies C, D, and S) are large companies with more than $1 billion in sales. Two (C and D) are included under (6) above. The third firm holds 7.8 percent of the patents and accounts for about 32 percent of the utilizations. Though it has used a large number of its government inventions, these inventions generally have played a supporting role. Only three represent significant sales, amounting to $3.0 million at the date of the survey.

(8) *Overall Effect of Policy on Utilization.* Notwithstanding the varing roles assigned patent rights by the firms described above, the key question is whether permitting them to retain exclusive rights will, on balance, promote utilization better than acquisition of title by government. The study data indicate that the answer is yes where the inventions as developed under government contracts are not directly applicable to commercial uses and the inventing contractor has commercial experience in the field of the invention. This occurs most frequently with DOD, NASA and AEC inventions. In the case of DOD, the fact that it does not actively promote commercial use of its patents is an added factor. In these instances the inventing contractor with commercial experience appears to be the logical candidate to attempt utilization either directly or by licensing others. The answer is also yes where the invention is commercially oriented but requires

substantial private development to perfect it, applies to a small market, or is in a field occupied by patent sensitive firms and its market potential is not alone sufficient to bring about utilization. Inventions in this category may arise with any agency and may have had only limited development toward a commercial application by the government itself.

2. Public-Service Agency Inventions

The public-service agency inventions all achieved utilization without exclusive rights. Utilization was achieved primarily because the inventions were highly commercial in nature and because they were extensively developed and promoted by the sponsor agencies.

a. *Commercial Nature of the Inventions.* The consumer orientations of the public-service agency inventions makes them more attractive to prospective users than inventions—such as those of DOD—which are not originally intended for public use. (The utilized inventions of public-service agencies are identified in Table 14.)[12] The inventions that achieved the greatest success—potato flakes developed by the Department of Agriculture and the fertilizer inventions of TVA—all are used in products having broad consumer demand. The sugar beet extraction process, another important Agriculture invention, provides the sugar beet extraction industry with a cheaper and more convenient process for extracting water in the manufacture of beet sugar. The dialdehyde starch inventions (Agriculture) have applications as wet-strength paper additives; the foam-mat process (Agriculture) provides one of the most inexpensive ways of dehydrating foods; the cotton opener provides a more efficient method for opening, cleaning, and blending cotton; and synthetic mica has a wide range of uses as a superinsulator in the electrical and electronic industries.

Even the inventions that have not been used are commercially oriented (Table 15). Among these are two processes for desalination of water, a mechanical crab-picker, a method for preserving walnuts, a process for flameproofing fabrics, a textile fiber cleaning machine, and a process for extracting oil from shale. As shown in Table 15, the reasons for their nonutilization are largely technical and relate to the invention's state of development.

b. *Role of Agency Mission—Development and Promotion.* It is not coincidental that these inventions originate with the public-service agencies since the

missions and R&D programs of these agencies are oriented toward the civilian economy. To the extent that they select their research to fulfill civilian needs, these agencies function—with one essential difference—like industrial firms looking for new markets: Since they are not required to earn a profit, they are freer than most industrial organizations to sponsor high-risk research with future, rather than imminent, utilization prospects. This pattern is particularly significant with Agriculture and TVA since their programs benefit conservative industries, such as food, textile, or fertilizer, which perform little of their own research or development. These agencies have become, to a large extent, the research arm of these particular industries. This relationship is noted in a number of the cases in Volume IV where the companies involved attribute lack of utilization to the government's failure to carry development of the invention far enough.

The extent of development undertaken by these agencies is a second major factor in achieving utilization of these inventions without exclusive rights. Research shows that the agencies have to develop the inventions extensively for commercial use before firms will attempt application without patent protection.

The Department of the Interior experience illustrates the importance of full development. Much of its research—particularly in water desalination, coal, and oil—is basic in nature and parallels work being performed by research- and development-oriented firms that are sensitive to patent rights. And although Interior's research has great commercial potential, the technology involved is speculative and commercially feasible inventions are still in the development stage. Industry has hesitated, in many instances, to undertake private commercial development of these inventions without patent protection. Here, nonexclusive rights have not been as effective as with Agriculture and TVA inventions. When research is performed under contracts, patent rights are often an issue (see Volume II, Part IV) and resulting inventions, because they are not yet economically feasible, do not spark wide interest in industry. Similar reactions are found in the government's health programs, discussed in Volume II, where drug firms will not use the results of HEW research if these results appear to conflict with their patent position.

Development alone, however, may not insure commercialization of public-service agency inventions without exclusive rights. Often intensive promotion is needed to convince potential users of the invention's commercial value. For example, the Department of Agriculture market tested potato flakes in supermarkets before food processors picked up the invention. TVA has had similar experiences with fertilizers it developed.

---

[12] Case studies of these inventions are presented in Volume IV, Part III.

TABLE 14
UTILIZED INVENTIONS
(PUBLIC-SERVICE AGENCIES)

Case	Sponsor Agency	Number of Government Patents Involved	Additional Inventions (Trade Secrets/Patents)	Licensees/ Utilizers	Investment[4]	Annual Market[5]
1. Dialdehyde Starch	Agriculture	8	Secrets and patents	1/1	About $2.5 million	About $750,000
2. Synthetic Mica	Interior	1	Secrets	2^1/2	About $2 million	About $600,000
3&4. Liquid and Mixed Fertilizer Process	TVA	4	None	130/many[1]	About $40,000	About $3 million
5. Cotton Opener	Agriculture	1	Secrets and patents	13/3[1]	About $40,000	About $140,000
6. Superphosphoric Acid	TVA	1	None	3/1	N/A[8]	N/A[8]
7. Sugar Beet Extraction	Agriculture	2	None	1/more than 1[2]	N/A[6]	N/A[6]
8. Foam-mat Process for Drying Foods	Agriculture	3	Patents	4/1	About $300,000	N/A[7]
9. Low-Temperature Phase Equilibria Cell[3]	Interior	1	Unknown	1/more than 1[2]	N/A[9]	N/A[9]
10. Potato Flakes	Agriculture	3	Patents	6 or more	Unknown	$8 million

[1] Case research on all licensees was not performed for the study. Number of licensees reflects licensees under most "popular" of patents involved in the product.
[2] Firms other than those licensed are believed to practice the invention.
[3] Government sources believe this invention to be in use although single licensee declined to be interviewed.
[4] Investment of "most successful" utilizers in case where more than one attempt took place.
[5] Current annual market of "most successful" utilizer.
[6] A process improvement invention used by a company with $40 million sales. No breakout of investment or contribution of invention available.
[7] Current market is only in pilot plant design and installation.
[8] A process for turning out an existing product–acid manufactured by new process probably amounts to several million dollars; investment estimates were not available.
[9] Only known utilizer declined to be interviewed.

Both agencies employ a variety of techniques to promote the use of new products which make industry aware of valuable innovations developed by the government and which stimulate demand.[13] Thus, it appears that, in most cases, three factors contributed to commercial utilization of these inventions without exclusive

[13] Promotional approaches by government agencies are, discussed in Volume III.

rights: The inventions were commercially oriented and there were a clear need and market demand for them; the government undertook extensive development of the invention in its commercial form; and the government promoted industry interest in the invention.

Several firms studied did achieve utilization of government-sponsored inventions without these three factors. These companies picked up inventions in various stages of government development and went on to devise

TABLE 15
NONUTILIZED INVENTIONS
(PUBLIC-SERVICE AGENCIES)

	Case	Sponsor Agency	Patents Involved	Licensees	Reasons for Nonutilization	Private Investment
11.	Solar Still	Interior	1	1	Only technical feasibility demonstrated; government now funding alternative methods	None
12.	Electrolytic Process for Desalination of Water	Interior	1	1	Development work not finished	None
13.	Hydrate Process for Desalination of Water[1]	Interior	5	1	Development work not finished; patent rights issue with firm	$495,000
14.	Centrifugal Compression Distillation	Interior	1	1	Utilization tried but severe technical problems encountered	Some[3]
15.	Shale Oil	Interior	1	1	No market need yet, although thought to have promise; patent rights problems	Some[3]
16.	A Calcium Carrying Agent for Medicinal Applications	Agriculture	1	1	Research not yet complete; thought to have promise	$100,000
17.	Gelsoy (Manufacture of Sausages)	Agriculture	1	1	Lack of availability of raw material: no USDA follow through	Some[3]
18.	Textile Fiber Cleaning Machine	Agriculture	1	4	Utilization tried but severe technical problems encountered	$20,000
19.	Flameproofing of Fabrics	Agriculture	5	5	Chemical and raw material problems	About $80,000[4]
20.	Coumarone Derivatives	Agriculture	1	1	Technical problems; reorganization of firm	None?
21.	Preservation of Walnuts	Agriculture	1	1	More practical alternative method developed concurrently	Some[2]
22.	Vinyl 9, 10-Epoxystearate	Agriculture	1	1	Chemical limitations and high cost relative to other methods	None
23.	Honeycomb (Uncapping Apparatus)	Agriculture	1	25	No market need; too complex for commercial application	None
24.	Deamidized Gliadin	Agriculture	1	1	No market need; licensee not in business related to potential use	
25.	Mechanical Crabpicker	Interior	1	2	Development unsuccessful to date	None

[1] This case also documented in Volume II.
[2] Development undertaken on cooperative basis with USDA (amounts not available).
[3] Records not available.
[4] Amount spent by only one of several commercial firms attempting to utilize.

new products based on the original patents. As shown in Table 14, these firms often gain protection by patenting improvements to the original invention or by trade and processing secrets growing out of their own research. Here, government patents, although not utilized in their original form, have stimulated private research that led to commercial products. The utilization achieved by this method is not readily measurable, but it is significant.

3. Transfer of Technology in the Nonprofit Environment

a. *Licensing Programs.* Inventions arising out of nonprofit research do not travel the same route to commercial utilization as inventions arising out of industrial research. While there is much variation in the policies and practices of educational and nonprofit research institutions, we found more similarities than differences among them when contrasted with industrial commercialization practices. The nonprofit institutions do not make or sell the products and processes embodying their inventions and must license these inventions in order to have them used. Therefore, these institutions have evolved a variety of licensing techniques to transfer technology from nonprofit research programs to the marketplace.

Some colleges and universities, such as those discussed in Volume IV, Part IV, Cases 1, 3, and 6 have their own licensing programs. These programs call for processing patents through special administrative units that are responsible directly to the administration of the senior policy-making group in the institution.

Other colleges and universities administer patents as a part of the routine duties of established offices and faculty committees. At the state university discussed in Case 2, for example, the dean of the graduate school is chairman of the patent committee. An office of research services, which is responsible for administration of sponsored research, provides the necessary administrative support. Here, as in other institutions which lack formal licensing programs, the administrative arm of the school ensures that pertinent institutional regulations are observed, that there is compliance with invention-reporting requirements of government contracts, and that the rights of the parties involved are guarded in the rare case of a decision to patent an invention.

Many educational institutions administer patent programs through independent foundations, for various legal, financial, and policy reasons that are only occasionally related to invention utilization. In these instances, the invention is assigned to the foundation either by the institution or by the inventor hemself. The technical institute in Case 6 and the liberal arts college in

Case 9 administer their patent programs in this way. The reasons for establishing such foundations include:

- Insulating patent funds from use by the state agency, or even by the university itself, for purposes other than financing scientific research;
- Creating a buffer between the nonprofit institution and industrial licensees in the event of litigation;
- Limiting contractual and tax liabilities;
- Providing a degree of flexibility in relationships between the nonprofits and industry not possible with the nonprofit institution alone;
- Facilitating a continuing relationship between the inventor and the licensee in order to develop the invention.

In many instances, a patent administration foundation was created to relieve the institutional administrative staff of the complicated and time-consuming technical and commercial problems of patent management. However, as additional duties were delegated, a number of the 50 to 60 such foundations retained patent development firms like those discussed in Cases 15 and 16, below, to manage their patent portfolios.

The principal agent for the transfer of the patentable products of nonprofit research to industry is the patent development firm. Of the 349 institutions described by Palmer,[14] 212 have contracts with patent development firms; in our investigation, all but three of the institutions having patent programs were also found to have contracts with such firms. Some patent development firms serve a restricted clientele or a limited technological market. Only three firms offer their services in invention marketing to all educational institutions, foundations, and nonprofit research corporations. The services of patent development firms include:

- Evaluation of disclosures.
- Assistance in preparation of patent applications.
- Negotiation of licenses.
- Distribution of royalties.
- Policing the patent.

The firms act as a clearinghouse for the nonprofits and as a marketplace for industry. Patents are typically assigned to the patent development firm on a royalty-sharing basis. Patent applications are filed on approximately 10 to 15 percent of the disclosures submitted and, if present circumstances continue, only one-quarter of these patents will ever be licensed.

---

[14] A comprehensive survey of the patent policies, practices, and procedures of universities, technological institutions, and nonprofit organizations was commissioned by the Patent Policy Survey of the National Research Council (National Academy of Sciences) in 1946. Dr. Archie M. Palmer published five monographs between 1952 and 1962 depicting the patent activities of the 945 institutions, with a description of the situation at each of the 349 institutions which conduct scientific and technological research and have invention policies.

b. *Characteristics of Inventions of Nonprofit Institutions.* Inventions arising out of nonprofit research have a distinctly different character than the patentable ideas arising from R&D contracts with industry. In nonprofit research, the end product is normally "software"—scientific findings—and patentable ideas take the form of concepts rather than hardware. In industry R&D, on the other hand, the result is usually "hardware"—a product, process, or component—and a working model, at least, will have been developed.

The task of a nonprofit organization is over and the contract has been fulfilled when the organization submits a research report. Funds are rarely available to reduce the discovery to any practical application, and interest and motivation to seek utilization are often also absent. The idea of following an invention through development and production to a marketable product is alien to the academic and nonprofit environment. For this reason, the patent licensing profession refers to academic invention as a "bare bones patent." Industry must take it from there.

In contrast, under comparable government research contracts, the industry contractor normally seeks to promote follow-on work that will further develop his findings—ultimately, into a product. Should contract research result in an invention with commercial possibilities, in-house funds may be assigned to develop and exploit it.

Nonprofit research inventions usually require a larger investment for commercialization than industry discoveries because nonprofit inventions are frequently at an earlier stage of development. In our investigation, the nonprofit institutions repeatedly emphasized the additional investment industry has made to develop products based on nonprofit discoveries. In Case 1, for example, the industrial licensee invested a quarter of a million dollars in the tomato harvester after eleven years of university research developed a patentable prototype. The patent development firm in Case 16 has already made a comparable investment in seeking applications of holography, and still the patented disclosures relate only to the mathematical theory of wavefront reconstruction, rather than to any marketable three-dimensional imaging device.

The institute in Case 3 has been extremely critical of development firms that license university patents to companies which are not prepared to invest the necessary development capital. In short, inventions from nonprofit concerns are grains of sand about which a pearl may be formed only if industrial development is undertaken.

Another characteristic of nonprofit inventions is that they stand alone. Their isolation is a major obstacle to utilization, since most inventions are not marketable products in themselves. (In only 55 inventions investigated by Harbridge House was the patented discovery regarded as critical to the product.) The industrial product is often protected by a cordon of patents, as illustrated by the list of patents on a packet of Polaroid film. A university invention, on the other hand, is a one-shot patent. Even if the patent specification discloses an ingenious invention, the patent claims which define the scope of the monopoly are likely to be narrowly drawn. Whereas industry will add to its patent arsenal as a product is improved, a university patent, if it is to be licensed at all, must be licensed on the initial effort. Thus, the patent development firm in Case 16 did not begin to see a return on an invention which revolutionized an industry until the basic patent had run for thirteen years. By then, however, the industrial developer had patented a line of industrial improvements over the basic invention.

Industry can profitably keep an innovation "on the shelf" until the time is right to market it. Furthermore, cross-licensing agreements between firms extend the economic utility of the industrial patent. Nonprofit inventions, on the other hand, remote from the market to begin with, are perishable if unlicensed, since the nonprofit organizations do not have manufacturing operations. All the above characteristics of inventions developed by nonprofit institutions make them high-risk commercialization ventures.

c. *Patenting Versus Publishing Research Results.* Another major factor which affects invention utilization by academic institutions is the drive to publish research results. This drive produces a dilemma where utilization of inventions is concerned, since patents are the only protection for the inventions of nonprofit institutions. In the nonprofit environment, there is no economically useful equivalent of "proprietary data" or industrial trade secrets. While industry may benefit from these alternatives to patenting, the secrecy involved is counter to the tradition in university and nonprofit research.

This tradition reflects the relative values academic institutions place on publishing and patenting the results of their work. Publications are central to scholarly pursuit. Invariably, the results of research, except those limited by the terms of a grant or contract, are fully disclosed through articles in scientific and technical journals. Patents, on the other hand, have traditionally been regarded as irrelevant at best and, at worst, as an indication of unworthy commercial motives. All but one of the educational institutions interviewed declared that publication of research results is preferred even if, by doing so, patentability of an invention is endangered.[15] Thus, we found that perhaps the single most difficult task of a university patent administrator was the solicitation of invention disclosures. Even if the inventor was willing to cooperate in the utilization process, it was a familiar story that the university patent office only learned of the invention eight months after publication in a scientific or technical journal.

Since, under the present law, patent applications must be filed within one year of public disclosure of the invention or the patent will be banned, patentable ideas are frequently lost to an institution's portfolio. The universities, however, have never considered the industrial alternative of delaying publication until a patent is filed, resting on the comfort of one year within which to file an application. The college officials in Case 10 proposed that the government agencies retain an option to prohibit publication during a contractual evaluation period rather than require clearance prior to publication.

While nonprofit institutions actively disseminate technology through publication, promoting utilization of a specific invention is another matter. Given the academic preference for publication of research results over patenting them, a major problem exists in mounting an effective patent promotion program. As the cases illustrate, except for a few universities and technical schools, there is today little active promotion of patents by academic institutions.

Notwithstanding the low-key promotion of inventions by academic institutions, the critical question concerning utilization is whether patents would be promoted more effectively through government ownership, given their speculative utility. Research indicates that the mission-oriented and mixed-activity government agencies—DOD, NASA, and AEC—would promote patents largely through publicity. These agencies would not, as a rule, develop inventions beyond the agency mission expressed in the contract. A chance overlap in government and commercial requirements then, determines the applicability of the inventions in the commercial market. In most cases, substantial private development is required to commercialize patents, and the nonexclusive license the above agencies would offer may not compensate for the development risks involved. Allowing academic and nonprofit institutions to keep title, under these circumstances, offers greater flexibility in providing patent protection to interested developers, when that is necessary to achieve utilization. Title also motivates the inventor to assist in developing the invention for commercial use, because of its potential rewards to him.

Inventions of public service agencies—such as TVA, HEW, and the Departments of Agriculture and the Interior—may differ from the inventions discussed above in two important respects: their close alignment with commercial needs, and their greater agency development and promotion for public use. Review of public service agencies[16] and their promotional programs suggests that TVA and Department of Agriculture inventions have a good chance of utilization if these agencies retain title, and invest in invention development and promotion. HEW and Department of the Interior inventions, on the other hand, require strong patent incentives for industry because of high product development costs and minimum agency development and promotion. For these inventions commercial utilization would appear to be better promoted by allowing academic and nonprofit institutions to retain title.

E. Speed of Utilization

Survey inventions that were utilized, for the most part, found quick application. Table 16 shows the time lag between patent application and first commercial utilization of contractor inventions. About a third of the inventions had been used commercially by the time a patent application was filed, and assuming three years for patent issue, about two-thirds had been used by the time a patent was received.

Prior experience plays an important role in the speed with which inventions are used. If rapid utilization is defined as occurring in three years or less from the date of application, inventions developed by firms with prior commercial experience achieved a ratio of 77 rapid to 15 slow utilizations (see Table 16). In contrast, firms without prior commercial experience had a ratio of only 31 to 22.

The mix of government and commercial business is a second major factor which affects speed of utilization. Firms in the middle range of government activity (20 to 80 percent government business) use inventions much more quickly than companies who are predominantly in the commercial or the government market. These middle range firms have a ratio of 47 rapid to 4 slow utilizations compared with 61 rapid to 33 slow for the other companies, due, at least in part, to the fact that firms with both low and high proportions of government activity separate their government and commercial work to a greater extent than do the firms in the medium range of government activity.

---

[15] Case 1 is a qualified exception to this rule.

[16] See Volume III, on government efforts to promote utilization.

TABLE 16
TIME LAG FROM PATENT APPLICATION TO FIRST COMMERCIAL UTILIZATION
CONTRACTOR ACTIVITY FOR SAMPLE YEARS 1957 AND 1962

Independent Variables	≤0 Years	1-3 Years	4-8 Years	≥9 Years	9* Years	Total
Sales of Firm						
Less than $5 million	3	4	2	0	3	9
$5 - $50 million	8	6	7	0	1	21
$50 - $200 million	5	11	3	3	6	22
Over $200 million	37	33	22	0	14	92
TOTAL	53	54	34	3	24	144
Prior Activity						
Yes	41	36	13	2	8	92
No	12	19	21	1	16	53
						145
Percent Government Business						
0-20	16	14	20	2	2	52
20-50	16	10	3	0	2	29
50-80	10	11	1	0	7	22
80-100	11	20	10	1	13	42
						145
Field of Technology						
Mechanical	14	22	12	1	6	49
Other	39	33	22	2	18	96
						145
Form of Invention						
Material	12	10	6	0	2	28
Process	2	4	0	0	3	6
Component	22	17	7	1	10	47
End Product	17	24	21	2	9	64
						145
Kind of Agency						
DOD	50	53	31	3	24	137
AEC	2	1	3	0	0	6
Other	1	1	0	0	0	2
						145

*Years between filing and first expected commercial utilization. This column is not included in the row totals.

F. Reasons for Nonutilization

The survey questionnaire asked contractors and licensees to enumerate reasons for nonuse of government inventions in which they had rights. In each case, responders were asked to rank 10 different reasons according to their importance in the decision not to utilize. Significant differences which appeared in the answers of contractors and licensees are summarized in Tables 17 and 18.[17]

1. Contractor Inventions

Contractors indicated that the low commercial potential of their government inventions is the greatest barrier to utilization. Over 70 percent of the first-ranked reasons in Table 17 are in this category.[18] These inventions are derived mainly from defense programs and most are too far removed from consumer needs to be truly useful commercially. Developed under hardware programs in many instances, they represent applied

[17] In Tables 17 and 18, the first row indicates the number of times a reason was ranked first, the second row, the number of times a reason was ranked second, and so forth.

[18] These reasons include no commercial potential seen (420), technology too sophisticated (171), expected market failed to materialize (208), and invention became obsolete (236).

TABLE 17
REASONS FOR NONUTILIZATION OF INVENTIONS
(CONTRACTOR INVENTIONS, 1957 AND 1962)

Frequency
Percent

Reason for No. Commercial Utilization	No Reason Given	Development Costs Too High	Development Revealed Serious Flaws	Development Personnel Not Available	Invention Became Obsolete	Expected Market Failed to Materialize	Technology too Sophisticated	Too Much Competition	Channels of Distribution Lacking	Invention Falls Outside of Company Product Line	No Commercial Potential Seen	All Other	Total Reasons Given
1	244	20 (1.4)*	21 (1.4)	6 (.4)	236 (16.2)	208 (14.3)	171 (11.7)	10 (.7)	26 (1.8)	234 (16.1)	420 (28.9)	102 (7.0)	1,454
2	1,116	80 (13.7)	23 (4.0)	4 (.7)	76 (13.1)	78 (13.4)	62 (10.7)	26 (4.5)	43 (7.4)	67 (11.5)	86 (14.8)	37 (6.3)	582
3	1,470	22 (9.6)	15 (6.6)	5 (2.2)	22 (9.6)	34 (14.9)	17 (7.5)	28 (12.3)	17 (7.5)	48 (21.0)	10 (4.4)	10 (4.4)	228
4	1,611	3 (3.4)	7 (8.1)	3 (3.4)	35 (40.3)	6 (6.9)	5 (5.8)	8 (9.2)	6 (6.9)	12 (12.7)	1 (1.5)	1 (1.5)	87
5	1,635	1 (1.6)	1 (1.6)	7 (11.1)	10 (15.9)	34 (54.0)	3 (4.8)	1 (1.6)	3 (4.8)	2 (3.2)	0 (0)	1 (1.6)	63

Rank of Reason

*Percentage is the total responses for a reason, divided by the total reasons given for that row.

TABLE 18

REASONS FOR NONUTILIZATION OF INVENTIONS
(NONINVENTOR LICENSEES OF GOVERNMENT-OWNED PATENTS, 1957 AND 1962)

Frequency
Percent

Reason for No Commercial Utilization (Rank of Reason)	No Reason Given	Development Costs Too High	Development Revealed Serious Flaws	Development Personnel Not Available	Invention Became Obsolete	Expected Market Failed to Materialize	Technology Too Sophisticated	Too Much Competition	Channels of Distribution Lacking	Invention Falls Outside of Company Product Line	No Commercial Potential Seen	All Other	Total Reasons Given
1	23	9 (13.1)*	16 (23.2)	0 (0)	8 (11.6)	5 (7.3)	3 (4.3)	0 (0)	0 (0)	19 (27.6)	2 (2.9)	7 (10.1)	69
2	53	6 (15.4)	2 (5.1)	2 (5.1)	2 (5.1)	4 (10.3)	1 (2.6)	0 (0)	1 (2.6)	5 (12.8)	3 (7.7)	13 (33.3)	39
3	74	1 (5.5)	2 (11.1)	0 (0)	2 (11.1)	2 (11.1)	6 (33.3)	0 (0)	1 (5.5)	1 (5.5)	0 (0)	3 (16.7)	18
4	80	0 (0)	1 (8.3)	0 (0)	1 (8.3)	7 (58.3)	1 (8.3)	0 (0)	1 (8.3)	1 (8.3)	0 (0)	0 (0)	12
5	82	1 (10.0)	0 (0)	1 (10.0)	6 (60.0)	1 (10.0)	0 (0)	0 (0)	0 (0)	1 (10.0)	0 (0)	0 (0)	10

*Percentage is the total responses for a reason, divided by the total responses given for that row.

engineering to meet a specific requirement and, thus, their application to other products is limited. Developed under more basic research in other cases, they are still too speculative to find quick commercial application. There are notable exceptions with high potential—transistors, vacuum tubes, numerical control devices, computers and gas turbine engines—as noted earlier in connection with sales, but the exceptions prove the rule since these inventions have commercial applications which closely parallel their government uses.

Table 19 which groups the reasons and responses in the two categories of technical and marketing shows the effect of prior experience, patent rights, percent government business, and size of firm on nonutilization. Of the four factors, patent rights have the greatest effect on whether nonutilization was attributed to technical or marketing reasons. Technical reasons for nonutilization rate 15 percent higher when the contractor has title than when he does not. Interviews with firms in the survey indicate that this is caused by contractors' normally not taking title when the inventions clearly appear to have no utility. Thus a marketing reason is inherent in the decision not to take title. Even where contractors own the patents, however, marketing reasons still predominate since contractors often take title when utilization is only a speculative possibility, resulting in ownership of many inventions with low commercial potential.

Table 19 also shows the parallel effect of prior experience and percent government business. With both factors, greater contact with commercial markets appears to increase the percentage of patents acquired that have commercial potential, resulting in a smaller number of inventions eliminated for marketing reasons.

2. Government-Owned Inventions

In contrast with contractors, licensees of government-owned inventions found development costs and development flaws rather than low commercial potential an important barrier to utilization. Those two reasons were ranked first in 35 percent of the responses (Table 18) compared with 2.8 percent for the contractor group (Table 17). The market orientation of the firm is also a more important factor with licensees than with contractors: That the invention was outside company product lines was ranked first in 27 percent of the licensee responses (Table 18), compared with 16 percent for contractors (Table 17).

Table 20 measures the effect of prior experience on licensees' reasons for nonutilization of inventions. Both with and without prior experience, technical reasons are more important to licensees (76.4 percent with experience and 50 percent without) than to contractors (39.7 percent with experience and 31.9 percent without—see Table 19). Licensees with prior experience, however, rate technical reasons more important than those without it. Interviews indicate that licensees without prior experience often inquire about an invention to determine if it is of commercial interest to them, normally receive a license in response to the inquiry, and, then upon closer examination of the invention, often conclude they do not wish to pursue it. Licensees with prior experience, on the other hand, tend to screen inventions in their field more carefully before inquiring about them, resulting in a higher proportion of marketing reasons for licensees without prior experience than for those who have it.

TABLE 19
FACTORS AFFECTING REASONS FOR NONUTILIZATION OF INVENTIONS

Utilization Factor	Technical Reasons for Nonutilization (percent)	Marketing Reasons for Nonutilization (percent)	Number of Observations
Contractor has prior experience.	39.7	60.2	405
Contractor has no prior experience.	31.6	68.3	958
Contractor has title.	35.9	64.0	1,187
Contractor has no title.	21.0	78.0	176
Contractor does more than 50% of his business with the government.	29.7	70.2	841
Contractor does less than 50% of his business with the government.	40.9	59.0	522
Contractor has annual sales over $50 million.	33.8	66.1	1,177
Contractor has annual sales under $50 million.	34.0	65.9	186

TABLE 20
EFFECT OF PRIOR EXPERIENCE ON REASONS FOR NONUTILIZATION
(GOVERNMENT-OWNED INVENTIONS)

	Technical Reasons (percent)	Marketing Reasons (percent)	Number of Observations
Prior Experience	76.4	23.6	17
No Prior Experience	50.0	50.0	44

PART IV. Effect of Government Patent Policy on Business Competition

A. Introduction

Reflecting the government's concern with maintaining a competitive economy, the patent study included tasks to determine whether government patent policy promotes or restricts business competition. Data on this question were gathered from four sources.

    (i) Questions on licensing were included in the utilization survey questionnaire to provide a data base for statistical analysis and case studies;

    (ii) A pilot study was conducted within the synthetic quartz crystal industry to determine the feasibility of using case studies to explain the effect of patent policy on competition;

    (iii) Case studies were conducted on sample patents involved in infringement suits to determine the effect on competition of inventions important enough to involve litigation; and

    (iv) Interviews were conducted with patentees who reported inventions unavailable for license to determine the importance of the inventions and their effect on competition.

In evaluating the impact of government patent policy on competition, it is important to distinguish the effects of patent policy from other effects which may result from industry participation in government programs. Competitive advantages in commercial markets may well accrue to government contractors through knowledge gained in new technologies, through sharpening of technical skills, and through government funding of R&D work, which has parallel commercial areas of interest. But these are quite separate from the advantages of owning patents to specific inventions. This study has tried to measure only the latter. And, it has tried to measure it in terms of the inventions included in the survey sample. While a broader study of the cumulative effect of government-sponsored inventions patented over several years might have provided more definitive data, we believe that the study data provides a representative and useful picture of the effects of patent policy on competition.

The study indicates that both in number of inventions utilized and in sales volume, the patents sampled appear to have had small impact on commercial markets. Although over 80 percent of both sample inventions and utilization were concentrated in 50 firms, only 55 inventions owned by contractors—2.7 percent of the sample—played a critical role in their commercial use, and five were responsible for $201 million out of the $406 million in cumulative sales attributable to contractor inventions. This utilization of critical-role contractor-owned inventions is low compared with the total sales of these firms and the industries in which they participate. Of equal importance is the fact that very few instances were reported where owners of government-sponsored inventions refused to license their patents. Only 15 inventions—less than 1 percent of the sample—involved such refusals, and these 15 refusals involved just five companies.

These statistics suggest that government patent policy has a very limited effect on business competition, a conclusion that is corroborated by the case data. None of the infringement suits investigated involved attempts by the patent owner to limit use of the patent to himself. On the contrary, the evidence is that the patent owner, despite a general willingness to license, may find his competitors using the patent first and negotiating a license only when he claims infringement.

The study did show that government retention of title, when coupled with full development and active government promotion of inventions having high commercial potential, has promoted competition. A striking example of this is the fertilizer industry where TVA developed high-concentrate fertilizers, patented them, proved their effectiveness on pilot farms and their commercial feasibility in pilot production, and aggressively promoted their use among farmers and fertilizer manufacturers. Industry sales have increased greatly through the manufacture of these fertilizers by many small regional producers. In circumstances like these, government retention of title can be an effective spur to competition because licenses are available to all comers. But several additional factors must be present for patent policy to have this effect. It must be evident to licensees that the invention has good commercial potential. The invention must be producible in commercial quantities and marketable at a cost that is competitive with alternative product. And the risks of recouping development costs must be no greater than similar investment opportunities available to the licensee.

In most cases, government agencies have to go far beyond discovery of an invention to create these conditions. Some agencies do—as described in the Volume III report on government efforts to promote utilization of government-sponsored inventions. The Department of Agriculture, for example, has an active program of developing inventions to the point of commercial feasibility. Potato flakes and frozen orange juice are two of its well-known successes. That agency, in promoting potato flakes, sponsored pilot production of the product and performed a market study in supermarkets in a major city to determine the product's consumer appeal. The study was then made available to the food industry to stimulate interest in the product.

Notwithstanding the utilization programs employed by government agencies, none except AEC has an express statutory mission to increase business competition in commercial markets for its own sake. When it does occur, however, it is an indirect result of their efforts to accomplish their basic mission. From our observations of the study inventions and insofar as the effect of patent policy is involved, competition does not appear to have been adversely affected by this lack of direct concern, for three reasons:

> (i) The rate of utilization of government inventions has been low.
> (ii) The agencies—such as TVA and Agriculture, whose inventions are most likely to be utilized— either developed them in-house or took title to them when developed under contract.
> (iii) And industrial owners of government-sponsored inventions have been willing to license them upon request or, where they were unwilling to license, alternative technologies were available to competitors in the great majority of cases.[1]

The sections below present additional findings which support these conclusions. Section B reports on the licensing of survey inventions and Section C discusses the survey patents involved in infringement suits.

B. Licensing of Inventions in the Utilization Sample

1. Licensing of Sample Inventions

The utilization survey indicated that responding industrial firms held exclusive rights on 1,618 patents in the utilization sample. Ninety-five percent—or 1,539 of the inventions—were reported to be available for license. The sample inventions generated 175 requests for license which resulted in 138 licensing agreements.[2] Industrial firms reported use of inventions by 77 licensees. Only 26

licenses covered inventions also used by the patentee and only eight were critically important in the patentees' use of them.

The small amount of licensing reported by patentees is consistent with the low level of commercial utilization among the survey inventions. The low levels of activity reflect, for the most part, the limited commercial value of most government-sponsored inventions. In comparison, one of TVA's fertilizer patents is used by at least 32 licensees, reflecting both its high commercial potential and the effectiveness of TVA promotional efforts. And, a DOD process patent for growing synthetic quartz is used by every firm in the synthetic quartz crystal industry.

Several utilization trends are apparent from the licensing data: The utilization rate for licenses is 5 percent of the inventions available for license[3]—about half the rate experienced through direct use of survey inventions. Measured against the number of license agreements, utilization is about 56 percent of the total,[4] reflecting the positive interest of licensees in inventions they wish to license.

Table 21 compares major aspects of contractor licensing activity. Although large firms (over $200 million) account for the major share of inventions available for license (79.9 percent), they account for a much smaller share of license requests (56 percent), license agreements (52.2 percent), and licenses in use (46.8 percent). This is due to the tendency of large firms to patent inventions more broadly for reasons such as to recognize employee inventions, to protect against infringement suits, to obtain patents with which to negotiate cross licenses in addition to patenting them for direct commercial utilization (see Volume IV, Part II). Thus, large firms have a larger share of inventions with speculative utility than do smaller firms.

This pattern is particularly pronounced for large firms doing 20 percent or less of their business with the government. This group accounts for 31.4 percent of the patents available for license, but it received only 5.7 percent of the license requests, and entered 3.4 percent of the licensing agreements. All that these firms did license, however, were used.

Large firms doing 80-100 percent of their business with the government show a contrasting pattern: Accounting for 18.5 percent of the inventions available for license, this group received 26.9 percent of the license requests, entered into 28.7 percent of the licenses, but accounted for only 14.3 percent of the licenses in use. However, 10 of their 11 licenses in use covered

---

[1] Except for several case studies which investigated the field of the sample patents involved, studies were not conducted on the effect of a series or cluster of related government-sponsored inventions developed over a period of years.

[2] These agreements were individually negotiated and were not the result of automatic cross-licensing arrangements. No estimates were provided for the extent to which sample inventions were used under cross-licensing agreements.

[3] 1,539 inventions available for license; 77 licenses in use.

[4] 138 license agreements; 77 in use.

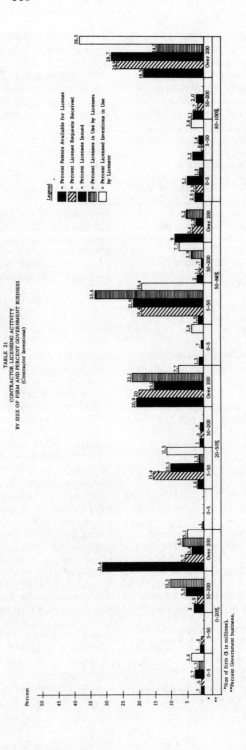

TABLE 21
CONTRACTOR LICENSING ACTIVITY
BY SIZE OF FIRM AND PERCENT GOVERNMENT BUSINESS
(Contractor Inventions)

Legend

■ = Percent Patents Available for License
▨ = Percent License Requests Received
■ = Percent Licensees Issued
▨ = Percent Licensees in Use by Licensees
□ = Percent Licensed Inventions in Use
    by Licensor

*Size of firm ($ in millions).
**Percent Government business.

inventions which the licensor was also using. Their performance clearly shows a willingness to license even where they use the inventions themselves.

By far the best licensing performance is achieved by firms with sales of $5 to $50 million doing 50 to 80 percent of their business with the government. They account for only 1.5 percent of the inventions available for license, but received 19.4 percent of the license requests, entered into 21.9 percent of the licenses, account for 33.8 percent of the licenses in use, and utilized directly five of the 26 inventions used by licensees. This group—which itself uses only 4.3 percent of the patents in commercial use—made its greatest contribution to utilization through licensing.

A consistent record of utilization both directly and through licenses is shown by large firms doing 20 to 50 percent of their business with the government: Accounting for 20.9 percent of the inventions available for license, they received 20 percent of the license requests, entered into 15.9 percent of the licensing agreements, and accounted for 22.1 percent of the licenses in use. This matches closely their *direct* utilization—27.5 percent of the survey inventions used.

2. Speed in Licensing

Speed in licensing contractor-owned inventions closely matches the speed with which contractors use the inventions themselves. The time lags between applications for patents and the dates of first license, as set forth in Table 22, show that 58 percent of the licensed inventions were licensed within three years of the application for a patent. This compares very favorably with the 68 percent used by patentees within that same period (see Table 16 above).

An even more meaningful test of diligence in licensing is the time it takes to reach agreement once a license request is received. A check of 13 respondents who reported a time lag of one year or more between first commercial use of an invention and issuance of license showed that all but one had issued licenses within one year of the request. In the latter case—involving a high-speed printer—we found no effort to delay licensing. The initial request was an informal inquiry for information. The requester then decided to purchase printers over the next year. When he did finally request a license, it was quickly granted.

3. Refusal to License

The utilization questionnaires were analyzed to determine the frequency and character of refusals to license survey inventions. A high rate of refusals would indicate

TABLE 22
TIME LAG BETWEEN PATENT APPLICATION AND FIRST LICENSE AGREEMENT MADE: CONTRACTOR ACTIVITY FOR SAMPLE YEARS 1957 AND 1962

Independent Variables	0-3 Years	4-8 Years	>9 Years
Size of Firm			
Less than $5 million	5	3	0
$5 - $50 million	12	2	0
$50 - $200 million	4	1	0
Over $200 million	26	23	4
T TOTAL	47	29	4
Prior Experience			
Yes	21	6	0
No	26	25	3
Percent Government Business			
0 - 20	3	3	0
20 - 50	9	6	0
50 - 80	9	2	0
80 - 100	26	18	4
Field of Technology			
Mechanical	12	8	0
Other	35	21	4
Form of Invention			
Material	3	3	0
Process	1	1	0
Component	21	17	1
End Product	22	8	3
Kind of Agency			
DOD	45	27	4
AEC	0	0	0
Other	2	2	0

that industry ownership of patents might have an adverse effect on competition. Initial analyses of the data identified 35 inventions as unavailable for license. All were investigated to determine the reasons for refusal.

Interviews revealed that 20 of the 35 inventions did not really involve refusals to license:

--Nine had either been sold outright or were involved in exclusive license agreements.

--Four were developed by companies which held only a license to the invention from the government.

--Seven involved questionnaires which were answered incorrectly and, consequently, were dropped from this aspect of the study.

The remaining 15 patents, involving five companies, reflected explicit management decisions to withhold licensing as part of their business strategy. (Table 23 lists pertinent information on these inventions.) Licenses were refused for two basic reasons: (i) to establish new markets for the company and (ii) to protect existing markets from competitors. One company, (Company 5), holding 8 of the 15 patents, categorically refused to license competitors when either of the above situations existed. The remaining four companies refused licenses selectively, depending upon their evaluation of the patents and specific market conditions. The first reason—establishment of new markets—was usually associated with specialized new products of limited applicability or with attempts to penetrate markets of well-entrenched competitors. The second reason— protection of existing markets—was a position generally adopted when the company was either competing

TABLE 23
REFUSALS TO LICENSE

	Invention	Company	Commercial Sales	Private Development Cost	Role of Invention	Reason for Refusal to License	Sponsoring Government Agency
(1)	Turbine drive mechanism for miniaturized jet fuel flowmeter	1	$1 million	$450,000	Supporting	Establish market position with new product	DOD
(2) & (3)	Design features and fluid seals for jet fuel flowmeter (two related inventions)	1	$800,000	$1 million	Supporting	Establish market position with new product	DOD
(4)	Porous metal and process for manufacture	1	$13,000	$300,000	Supporting	Establish market position with new product	DOD
(5)	Gas turbine motor scroll structure	2	$60 million	Not Available	Critical	Avoid direct competition	DOD
(6)	Punch guide for microfilm mounting	3	$500,000	$30,000	Supporting	Avoid direct competition	DOD
(7)	Bead breaker for tire mounting machine	4	$66,000	$2,000	Critical	Avoid direct competition	DOD
(8)	Electromagnetic pump for liquid metals	5	$1.25 million (commercial and government)		Supporting	Avoid direct competition	DOD
(9)	Reagent for carbon dioxide analysis	5	$11,000 (commercial and government)	Not Available	Critical	Avoid direct competition	DOD
(10)	Safety helmet with eye shield	5	Negligible	Not Available	Supporting	Avoid direct competition	DOD
(11)	Gas detection techniques	5	No commercial sales anticipated	Not Applicable	Not Applicable	Avoid direct competition	DOD
(12)	Shaft seal for liquid metal pumps	5	No commercial sales anticipated	Not Applicable	Not Applicable	Avoid direct competition	DOD
(13)	Contaminant analysis for liquid metals	5	No commercial sales anticipated	Not Applicable	Not Applicable	Avoid direct competition	DOD
(14)	Apparatus to maintain low oxygen atmosphere	5	No commercial sales anticipated	Not Applicable	Not Applicable	Avoid direct competition	DOD
(15)	Head positioner for helmet	5	No commercial sales anticipated	Not Applicable	Not Applicable	Avoid direct competition	DOD

against industrial giants or attempting to retain its market share through product superiority.

Nine of the 15 were used commercially (inventions 1 through 9, Table 23). Only three played a critical role in their commercial use. The most successful of these was a gas turbine motor scroll structure (invention 5, Table 23) which was critical to a gas turbine motor involving commercial sales of $60 million to date. The patentee has several active competitors in the gas turbine field and there are alternative ways of performing the function involved in this patent. Given the competitive conditions in this market, the company does not wish to make its design expertise available through license of the patent.

The other two critical inventions involved very modest sales. The first—a device which breaks a tire bead away from the wheel rim on an aircraft landing gear (invention 7, Table 23)—was developed under Navy contract and was an outgrowth of a smaller model which the contractor had invented, patented, and produced for many years. The invention played a critical role in expanding the commercial application of the bead-breaker and was directly responsible for sales of about $66,000. Nominal development costs of $2,000 were required to commercialize the device. Since the device is specialized and has a limited market, the patentee has no interest in encouraging entry of a competitor into the market by licensing the invention. The second—a reagent for analysis of carbon dioxide (invention 9, Table 23)—generated sales of only $11,000, both commercially and to the government.

The six other inventions which were commercially used played supporting roles in their commercial products. Three, relating to various design aspects of jet fuel flow-meters (inventions 1 to 3, Table 23), represent improvements in a basic patent already owned by the company. The patentee did not wish to license the inventions because it was trying to penetrate a market with a new product. The company invested $1.45 million to commercialize the product, and since 1962 when the invention was first put on the market, commercial sales have been $1.8 million.

This same company owns the fourth invention which played a supporting role—a process for the manufacture of formed metal of uniform density and pore size (invention 4, Table 23). It has been trying to commercialize the invention since 1950 at a cost of $300,000. The company refused a request for license in 1963 because it wished to develop the market from a protected position. But since it has been over five years since receipt of the patent and very little commercial utilization has been achieved—to date, commercial sales have amounted to $13,000—the company expects to turn the invention over to its licensing group for licensing to other manufacturers.

The fifth invention relates to an apparatus for cutting microfilm strips and matting them on aperture cards (invention 6, Table 23), and is part of microfilm processing equipment manufactured by the patentee. The company considers the machine to be highly specialized with only a limited market. Since commercial sales during the past 10 years have only amounted to some $500,000, the company feels quite capable of handling the entire future demand for the equipment and is not interested in licensing competitors. The company has invested some $30,000 in the invention to commercialize it. The sixth invention—a safety helmet with eye shield (invention 10, Table 23)—has had negligible sales.

The last company interviewed showed a somewhat different pattern than the companies discussed above. It refuses to license patents in any new or existing markets in which it is interested. Thus, none of the eight inventions it owns in the sample are available for license. Only three of these (inventions 8, 9, and 10, Table 23, described above) had any commercial sales. The company anticipates no commercial sales of the remaining five patents, which include a shift seal for liquid metal pumps, contaminant liquid metals, an apparatus to maintain low oxygen atmosphere, gas detection techniques, and a head positioner for a helmet.

Table 24 shows the effect of the size of the firm on these refusals to license. Only 1 percent of the inventions of larger firms (over $50 million) were unavailable for licenses compared with 7.6 percent for smaller firms. With respect to utilized inventions, smaller firms again kept a larger percentage for their own use (13.0 percent) than did larger firms (3.8 percent).

TABLE 24
EFFECT OF SIZE OF FIRM ON REFUSAL TO LICENSE

	License Available (Percent)	License Not Available (Percent)
Size of Firm		
Under $50 million	92.4	7.6
Over $50 million	99.0	1.0
Size of Firm Where Invention Is in Use		
Under $50 million	87.0	13.0
Over $50 million	96.2	3.8

However, the total number of refusals in the survey is negligible, and with the exception of the gas turbine motor scroll structure, none of the inventions described above made any appreciable impact on a commercial market. Even the turbine motor scroll was competing with alternative methods of performing the same function. There is little evidence in the survey inventions that refusals to license have had a material effect on business competition in commercial markets.

C. Sample Patents Involved in Lawsuits

1. Research Approach

Anticipating that patents involved in court proceedings were likely to be important and have a significant commercial impact, sample patents involved in law suits were investigated to identify inventions which have a significant effect on competition. The purpose, however, was not to study the law suits in themselves, but to determine the effect of the patents on competition.

Working from the listing of contractor-owned patents issued in 1957 and 1962 and from the patent sections of *Shepard's Citations* (including current supplements through July 1967[5]), we identified patents which had been involved in lawsuits between private parties regarding infringement or validity. The search of *Shepard's Citations* disclosed 16 private suits involving 11 patentees or assignees.

Next, the court files of these lawsuits were examined to determine the nature of the dispute and to decide whether the cases were relevant to the study.[6] In this step, four patents and six suits were eliminated because the main issues did not involve the patents, but were primarily claims for appropriation of trade secrets—one involved use of a patented invention under a government contract rather than commercial utilization. The remaining nine patents involving seven patentees or assignees were selected for further study. In addition, a tenth patent was added during the course of our research. Issued in 1960 to a firm already under study, it had far greater importance than the two related 1957 patents which were the starting point for the research. In each

case, interviews were conducted with patentees or assignees to obtain information about the inventions, their commercial development, their licensing and use, and their effect on business competition.

Much of the data provided to us by the companies interviewed were given in confidence. We have, therefore, disguised both the inventions and the companies involved and reported them only in summary fashion. For identification, we give the following titles to the cases:

    (i) Case 1 – The Small Business Case
    (ii) Case 2 – The Sophisticated Devices Case
    (iii) Case 3 – The Impressive Patent Case
    (iv) Case 4 – The Ninety-Percent Government Business Case
    (v) Case 5 – The Declining Business Case
    (vi) Case 6 – The Commercial Company Case
    (vii) Case 7 – The Nonprofit Institution Case
    (viii) Case 8 – The Critical Process Patent Case

2. The Patents Involved in Lawsuits

a. *The Small Business Case.* The invention involved in "The Small Business Case" is a critical component of a capital equipment item which sells for from $25,000 to $35,000 and which is the primary product of the company. The patentee is an individual inventor—a type who is sometimes thought to no longer exist in this era of group research by large companies—who owns a small business. His company has about 65 employees and has an expected sales volume for fiscal year 1967 of between $700,000 and $1 million, a record for the firm.

The patentee has licensed two domestic firms and the patent is available for license to others. The licenses include a complete transfer of technology. An infringement suit to collect royalties is in process against the largest firm in the industry. There is a widely used alternative technology to the invention and there are other more inexpensive ways of accomplishing its functions that have advantages in some applications.

b. *The Sophisticated Devices Case.* The invention in "The Sophisticated Devices Case" is a critical component of a specialty device which has its main use on government work, but which also has some sophisticated commercial applications that contribute annual sales of about $200,000 to the patentee. The firm has been trying to promote utilization of the invention commercially, a major factor in deciding to form a small subsidiary company to manufacture it and other less sophisticated devices (amounting to about 80 percent of the commercial market in the total product line) that are in the same product line. The commercial market for the

---

[5] The patent law requires that when a patent is the subject of a court suit, the Clerk of Courts must notify the Commissioner of Patents, who, in turn, publishes this information in "The Official Gazette." *Shepard's Citations* picks up these listings from "The Patent Gazette" and publishes a complete listing of the patents with citations to the court suits.

[6] No patent was adjudicated in any of these proceedings. While there were some interlocutory opinions and hearings on such matters as change of venue, all the proceedings, except those still continuing at the date of our research, were settled by the parties through stipulation of settlement, withdrawal, or voluntary dismissal.

sophisticated device has not yet developed to the extent the patentee expected. The company has licensed three domestic firms to use the invention, including its major competitor.

c. *The Impressive Patent Case.* The invention in "The Impressive Patent Case" is the most important patent of the ten studied. The invention is basic to a product line of capital equipment that has total annual industry sales of $22 million to $30 million. About 70 percent of this market is now government, but commercial sales are increasing. No alternative technology to the invention appears available.

The patentee does not manufacture the invention itself, but has entered into an exclusive license with a large diversified manufacturer, who is estimated to account for about 50 percent of the market. The exclusive licensee has negotiated two sublicenses with its major competitors and another two are close to agreement.

The exclusive licensee also manufactures a less sophisticated device in the same general product line covered by another basic government-sponsored patent not included in the sample. The two products compete in the market. Some 10 manufacturers produce the less sophisticated device, one of which has the major share of the market and was the first to sublicense the more sophisticated device.

d. *The Ninety-Percent Government Business Case.* "The Ninety-Percent Government Business Case" involves three patents owned by a patentee who is among the 50 largest defense contractors and does no commercial work in the field of the patent. Two of these, improvement patents issued in 1957 for which there is a significant amount of alternative technology, are available for licensing and are part of a broad cross-licensing agreement.

The third patent—issued in 1960—is the second most important one studied. It has been basic to important and expensive commercial applications involving sales to date of some $20 million. The patentee has licensed six manufacturers and one user; one manufacturer was included under a broad cross-licensing agreement.

e. *The Declining Business Case.* The patentee in "The Declining Business Case" has had declining commercial and military sales in the field covered by the two improvement patents involved in the study, even though it owns basic patents in the product line. The company's overall sales have also declined over the last several years.

Although the two improvement patents are available for licensing, there have been no requests from interested firms. The patentee's three basic patents and others in this field, however, have been licensed to its major competitor under a broad cross-licensing agreement. The two improvement patents were issued after the cutoff date of that agreement and were, therefore, excluded from it. An infringement suit is in process in a foreign country to collect royalties on the improvement patents.

f. *The Commercial Company Case.* The patentee in "The Commercial Company Case" applied its knowledge in a commercial field to develop a device for an entirely different application for the Department of Defense. It then applied the resulting invention—along with some other basic patents it owned—to a system used by one of its major commercial activities. Every competitor in the industry except one uses the patented equipment under license from the patentee.

g. *The Nonprofit Institution Case.* The patentee in "The Nonprofit Institution Case," is a nonprofit institution connected with a university. The organization does no manufacturing. The invention is critical to a device having modest market potential. When companies began using the invention commercially, the patentee made the decision to collect royalties under license, if possible, rather than dedicate the invention to the public and has licensed the invention to four companies.

h. *The Critical Process Patent Case.* The patentee in the "Critical Process Patent Case" does not practice the invention commercially, but has granted an exclusive license instead. The invention is critical in synthesizing an important mineral used in the electronic industry. The process makes the synthetic mineral produceable at a cost which is competitive with the natural product and, as such, has been instrumental in creating a small, but growing industry. The exclusive licensee is willing to license others, but at a royalty which may make their operations unprofitable. The validity of the patent is currently being tested in a suit involving an infringing user.

3. The Effect of Litigated Patents on Competition

a. *General Conclusions.* Each situation studied is unique but the general conclusion is that healthy competition exists in all of the cases involving litigated patents. There appears, at first blush, only one situation—"The Impressive Patent Case"—in which there might be enough economic leverage to raise concern over concentration. But even there the total dollar amount of industry sales in an increasing market is relatively small in comparison with the dollar volume of sales in other major industry product lines. As noted previously in "The Impressive Patent Case," five companies occupy the market for the equipment, and the exclusive licensee has at least one half of the market. We believe that the current degree of concentration arose from circumstances other than the fact that patent title was retained by the original R&D contractor:

—— The exclusive licensee obtained an early start in the technology. Even before it began negotiations for the exclusive license, it was working on a machine which performed many of the functions of the patented equipment to be used in its own internal manufacturing operations. The exclusive licensee, after receiving its license, completed the first production application of equipment embodying the invention and gained further momentum when it received a substantial government order for the equipment.

—— The combination of technological and marketing talents required to produce and market the equipment limited the attractiveness of producing the equipment to a few firms.

—— The stated licensing policy of the exclusive licensee is to license all comers on reasonable terms.

—— Government business still occupies about 70 percent of the market.

—— Improvement patents in the field are held by various companies.

—— The wide market for less sophisticated equipment not covered by the subject patent is part of the competitive environment of the sophisticated equipment because buyers may choose between these two types of equipments for many applications and among the 10 or so manufacturers of the less sophisticated equipment. The exclusive licensee does not have the major share of that market for the less sophisticated device.

In the "Critical Process Patent Case," the invention appears to give the exclusive licensee sufficient leverage to control the industry. We believe it is untypical of government inventions in this respect. But, provision for government "march-in-rights" to require licensing at reasonable rates would appear to provide the necessary safeguard to protect against the occurrence of such cases.

Similarly, the effect on competition of the other cases studied can be summarized as follows:

(i) *"The Small Business Case."* The activities of the small business in this case have increased competition and lessened concentration within its business area. The company's licenses have involved a full-scale transfer of technology.

(ii) *"The Sophisticated Devices Case."* The commercial market in this case is small, sophisticated, and, in large part, experimental; and government sales are four times commercial sales. Whereas the patentee has the major share of the government and commercial markets, the potential economic leverage of the invention is small since the patentee has licensed its major competitor and two others at low royalty rates.

(iii) *"The Ninety-Percent Government Business Case."* The patentee of this invention does not manufacture it and would like to see as many other firms as possible use the invention. Therefore, it has licensed six manufacturers and one user, and would license others. In addition, firms have used the invention rather freely without obtaining a license.

(iv) *"The Declining Business Case."* Since new companies have been entering this market during the life of the patent and the company's business in the market has declined, it is clear that the patent ownership has not had an adverse effect on competition or concentration.

(v) *"The Commercial Company Case."* Competition was not adversely affected in this case since the entire industry is licensed and the other commercial patents that the patentee developed were equally basic to the system.

(vi) *"The Nonprofit Institution Case."* The patentee here does no manufacturing and would like to see as many companies as possible use the invention. Over the life of the patent, four firms have desired to develop the equipment and have received licenses.

b. *Licensing Terms.* Licensing, of course, is a very important factor in the conclusions outlined above. Although many aspects of existing licenses, licensing policies, and royalties were discussed in the research at the various companies, copies of licenses were not available for examination. Much of this information is considered confidential by the companies interviewed.

Some firms did, however, reveal royalty rates. In "The Small Business Case," one license included a 5 percent royalty, based on the net selling price of the equipment. Another license, now inactive, required a 3 percent royalty on manufacturing and sale of the invention and 1 percent on the entire device embodying the invention. Licensees had strong bargaining positions here and were able to negotiate low royalty rates.

Another firm stated that royalty rates in its existing licenses are 3 percent to 5 percent and that the method of computing the royalty is based on a customary industry formula. In "The Critical Patent Process Case" a 10 percent royalty is requested by the exclusive licensee and some firms in the industry indicated that such a rate could make their work unprofitable.

Representatives of other firms made more general statements about royalty patterns and rates. In "The Impressive Invention Case," the patentee stated, "we license all comers at reasonable rates." The sublicense agreements are fixed-sum agreements payable over a period of years, and the exclusive licensee pays a certain royalty to the patent owner on each item it manufactures as well as a share of the sublicense royalty payments it receives.

With regard to licensing policy, all firms represented that licenses were available for licensing or—perhaps more realistically—that, "If it comes to our attention that someone is using or wants to use the patent, we will do something about it." This remark appears to reflect industrial patent situations more accurately than the statement that a patent is available for licensing. Often a patent owner is in the frustrating position of having to find out who is infringing on his patent in order to attempt to obtain royalties. This certainly was the case in "The Ninety-Percent Government Business Case" and in "The Nonprofit Institution Case" and "The Small Business Case" as well.

Several factors contribute to this situation. A number of firms take the attitude, "Why not use a patent, as necessary, before negotiating a license, since most patent suits are settled out of court and preliminary injunctions are rarely granted?" and the ideal corporation in which engineers and patent attorneys review all corporate actions for infringement of the patent rights of others does not widely exist. This situation changes the competitive environment from one in which the patentee may limit use of the invention to one in which he may have to aggressively seek out potential infringers.

On the other hand, the tendency to go sailing into infringement situations is certainly not universal. In connection with the two most important patents in our cases, for example, the same large firm was the first to be licensed because it expressed awareness of the patent to the patentee and initiated negotiations for a license. The licensee is widely known to have a patent policy based on deliberate action and advance planning.

Research showed that license negotiations can be very complex. To establish the proper royalty base and to decide what patents are to be included in the license, large companies having numerous divisions or subsidiaries may engage in protracted bargaining. Such bargaining did occur in a number of the selections considered. In one case, delay was encountered in arriving at a proper royalty base and, in another, in working out arrangements suitable for various divisions of the licensee. In a third case, a pending merger of the licensee caused delay. Moreover, in some of the cases, lengthy negotiations were terminated, and resulted in a lawsuit.

c. *Extent of Private Development to Commercialize the Inventions.* Four of the cases involved are inventions used in capital equipment sold in both commercial and military markets.[7] In all four of these cases the commercial application of the invention could have been anticipated at the time of invention disclosure. In this respect, these cases run contrary to assumptions often made about commercial use of items developed under military contracts. A fifth case[8] also involves general purpose capital equipment that has wide use in many industries, but the military use is specialized and does not have major commercial possibilities.

One would expect that only a small amount of private investment would be necessary to commercialize an invention whenever it can be used in the same basic configurations for both the government and commercial markets. The small business and declining business firms indicated that this expectation is correct; however, the exclusive licensee in "The Impressive Patent Case" reported that each firm that entered the field spent substantial amounts of private funds to bring the invention to market.

Another way of looking at the question of private investment is to ask, "Would the invention have been commercialized to the same extent once it was patented if the government had retained title?" It appears that in all but "The Sophisticated Devices Case" this would have been so, but this does not answer the question of whether the licensees under those circumstances would promote the invention as aggressively as when they had title. Also, the lack of patent protection may have its greatest adverse effect on small firms; the inventor in "The Small Business Case" would have been in a precarious position if he had not had the protection of the patent and its royalty income to support his entry into a market of much bigger competitors. Based on all observations of the sample inventions, little evidence was found that permitting contractors to retain title to government-sponsored inventions had an adverse effect on business competition.

---

[7] "The Small Business Case," "The Impressive Patent Case," "The Declining Business Case," and "The Nonprofit Institution Case."

[8] "The Ninety-Percent Government Business Case."

PART V. Effect of Government Patent Policy on Industry Participation in Government R&D Programs

A. Introduction

The effect of government patent policy on industry participation in R&D programs was the most difficult factor to measure because of the difficulty of obtaining data on the question. However, a useful understanding of problems in this area was obtained by studying the medicinal chemistry program of the National Institutes of Health (HEW) and various contracts of the Department of the Interior. This aspect of the study attempted to answer such questions as:

(i) Do competent business organizations refuse to undertake government R&D work—either entirely or in selected areas—because of government patent policy?

(ii) What effect does policy have on application of a contractor's most advanced private technology to government programs?

(iii) Does patent policy have any influence on the flow of information concerning new developments between a contractor's government and privately sponsored work?

The data available to us only allows us to define some first-order effects of the policy in this area.

Industry's main concern about participating in government research has been the compromise of private investment in research and invention. Frequent objection was made to the "peephole" effect of government programs, whereby the government receives rights in the accumulated results of private work. The "peephole" effect has its counterpart in patent matters where an invention has been conceived at private expense, but reduced to practice under a government program. The traditional patent provisions classify this as a government invention and dispose of its rights under the terms of the contract.

The reach of the contract has been extended in some programs to background patents owned by the contractor at the time of contracting. This practice causes the sharpest industry reaction of all because firms feel caught between their wish to participate in government programs and the need to protect their private investment and competitive position.

The major adverse effects of patent policy on participation are program delay, loss of participants, diversion of private funds from government lines of research, and refusal to use government inventions and research when questions regarding a company's proprietary position are raised. These adverse effects occur selectively, but they have occurred at important points in government programs observed in the study.

The key to the participation question, however, lies in the attitude of prospective contractors toward the role of patents in their activities. As noted in connection with utilization, patents have varying importance to organizations doing business with the government. Industrial firms whose major business objective is participation in government work and systems-oriented companies in the study sample were at one end of the scale and were found to assign patents a secondary role compared with technical and management competence. Patents typically were used by the former to provide recognition to technical personnel and to project the creative quality of their work to their government customers. Systems firms, on the other hand, were found to rely on patents to ensure design freedom, provide material for cross licensing agreements as well as to recognize creativity in their technical personnel. The data indicates that firms in these two categories are not likely to refuse to participate in government R&D for patent reasons. However, systems firms may encounter participation problems at the subcontract level if the government acquires title to all inventions developed under its program.

On the other hand, firms which place a high value on patents for defensive purposes tend to choose among the areas in which they are willing to undertake government research and may decline to participate in programs which impair their operational flexibility. And, firms in research-intensive industries like electronics and new technically-oriented firms seeking to develop a proprietary product-line through government research were found to rely on patents to establish proprietary positions. These firms tend to be selective in their government-sponsored research and may decline to participate in programs which conflict with their privately sponsored research and development or which do not promote their growth objectives for proprietary lines.

Firms which follow this policy even more fully try to assure corporate ownership of patents before initiating work on a government contract or may consciously isolate government work from their commercial operations. In the latter case, there is usually little interchange of technical innovations between the government and commercial activities of the firm and there may be some loss of relevant technical experience and applications to the government work.

Lastly, large diversified firms often follow different patent policies in different divisions of the organization. Accordingly, they may be willing to participate in government programs with small concern for patents in some areas but with great concern for patent rights in others. It is difficult to generalize about these firms except to notice that their policies tend to follow the patterns of the industries in which their divisions participate. Their behavior may, therefore, resemble any of the categories of firms described above if their divisions have similar business profiles.

With respect to educational and nonprofit institutions refusal to participate for patent reasons is not normally a problem. However, instances were found in Department of Interior programs where patent problems were encountered because of conflicting institutional obligations arising from joint support of a research program or where rights in background patents were sought as a condition of the project. With the rising interest in nonprofit institutions in patents as a source of revenue, greater concern over patent rights can be expected from institutions with large research programs as financial pressures on these organizations continue to increase.

Viewing the participation problem from the standpoint of individual government agencies, the effect of patent policy varies with the nature of their R&D programs and the contractors that participate in them. Participation problems are not a concern to TVA which performs virtually all its research and development itself and, therefore, has little or no contractual interface with industry. They are also minimal in Agriculture programs since that agency contracts almost all its extramural research and development with educational and nonprofit institutions. In addition, the firms that do participate in its programs do relatively little research and development on their own and tend to be less patent conscious than those participating in defense/aerospace work.

The direct effect of policy on NSF and HEW programs also appears to be small because most of their contract research is either basic in nature, offering limited opportunities to develop patentable inventions, or is performed by nonprofit institutions who, for the most part, are interested in the research for itself. However, some problems may be encountered in instances of joint or overlapping research at nonprofit institutions where the rights of other parties may be involved. And, a significant indirect effect has been noted in an important HEW health program where voluntary noncontractual participation by a patent sensitive industry was curtailed because of patent considerations.

The Department of Interior, like HEW and NSF, has a number of programs—such as water desalination—which are oriented toward basic research. The Agency contracts in these areas with research-oriented industrial firms (many of whom are patent conscious), as well as educational and nonprofit institutions, and acquires title to patents arising under its programs. Under some programs, statutes on which they are based have been interpreted to require the agency to acquire rights in existing patents owned by contractors because of their relevance to the contract effort and future utilization of contract results. These factors—patent conscious organizations and acquisition of rights to contract inventions and existing patents—have resulted in several instances of hesitation or refusal to participate in the government program. Insufficient data was available to establish how widespread the reaction was or its overall effect on Interior programs.

The largest number of opportunities for participation problems occur, of course, in DOD, NASA and AEC programs because of the size and scope of their contract effort. Only a limited amount of data was available on this question for these agencies but a few general observations may be made. At least as to the majority of DOD inventions, to which contractors are normally permitted to retain title, no problem arises. In addition, NASA's policy of waiving title to inventions to promote utilization under appropriate circumstances provides a method for resolving competing government and industry objectives with regard to patents arising under contract. Lastly, interviews with industrial firms in the survey sample indicate that—except where a large investment in related private research, know-how, inventions and/or patents considered to be important in commercial markets exist—acquisition or improvement of technical skills is sufficiently important to them in most cases to justify participating in government programs in their areas of interest even though patent provisions are not completely suitable to them.

However, this does not mean that either a title or license policy will equally serve the government's interests under all the above circumstances, since the policy selected may also affect industrial decisions to use contract inventions commercially. Here again, a balancing of government objectives appears necessary to ensure that the net effect of the patent policy promotes the government's overall goals.

B. Effects of Government Patent Policy on a Major Government Program

1. Lack of Collaboration in the National Institutes of Health (NIH) Medicinal Chemistry Program

The NIH medicinal chemistry program was studied by Harbridge House as an example of a major government program in which patent considerations were known to have a noticeable adverse industry-wide affect. Through this study it was possible to define the range of effects patent policy can have when the government either takes title to government-sponsored inventions or reserves the right to do so in programs involving a highly patent-sensitive industry.

The two key factors shaping industry reaction to the medicinal chemistry program are heavy private investment in civilian-oriented research which parallels government work, and application of that research to commercial products in which patents are important in establishing and maintaining a market position. When both these factors are present, patent policy may have a significant effect on participation in government programs and utilization of their patentable research results. A third factor—the extent of invention development by the government for commercial use—will also influence industry reaction even when the other two factors are present since it conditions the financial risks and potential rewards of using an invention without exclusive rights. In this respect, new compounds developed under the medicinal chemistry program are typically far removed from commercial products even when they show useful biological activity, and require substantial additional development beyond the work sponsored by the government. The sections below describe the effects of patent policy on both participation by the pharmaceutical industry in the medicinal chemistry program and its utilization of program results. Even though industry participation, prior to 1962, was provided at no cost to the government, we believe the effects of patent policy described below would have been the same if the government had attempted to acquire these services from industry under contract.

The NIH conducts extensive work in medicinal chemistry as part of its program in medical and health-related research. Normally 500 to 800 medicinal chemistry grants are in operation at any given time, and they annually account for about $8 million of the NIH grant program. Under these grants, new compounds believed to have potential medical value are developed; chemical synthesis techniques are studied; the relationship of chemical structure to biological activity is investigated; and research opportunities to promote professional development of medicinal chemists are provided. The typical grant is conducted by personnel associated with universities or hospitals and may cover a period of several years. Frequently, many related compounds are synthesized and tested under a single grant.

Prior to 1962 pharmaceutical firms had routinely made tests for biological activity—at no charge—on compounds developed by grantees. Such screening, required to establish the usefulness of the compounds, is the first step in developing new drugs. According to estimates furnished NIH by the pharmaceutical firms, screening a compound to the point where sufficient data are available to support a Federal Drug Administration application may cost $200,000 to $500,000. Most compounds do not survive the initial broad screening, which may only cost several hundred dollars or less depending on the tests performed.

Since many significant discoveries in medicinal chemistry have occurred by accident rather than by plan, the practice is to screen large numbers of compounds for a wide range of possible uses. The NIH medicinal chemistry program thus provides a fertile source of new and potentially useful compounds for pharmaceutical firms to explore. HEW patent policy has required that all rights in inventions arising out of NIH-sponsored research shall be determined by HEW. Prior to 1962, however, drug firms were never required to sign agreements with the grantee of NIH regarding rights to inventions discovered in screening.

In 1962 NIH began requiring pharmaceutical firms to sign a patent agreement before being permitted to screen compounds developed under NIH funds. The agreement imposed four conditions on the screener:

(i) It shall not disclose the results of testing for 12 months, except with the consent of all parties concerned.

(ii) It shall promptly report the results of testing to the investigator and will furnish him the information demonstrating any utility or new use of the compound for use by the PHS in connection with any application for patent that organization may file.

(iii) It shall be permitted to obtain patent rights to new uses of the compounds developed at its own expense *except* under three circumstances:

    (a) Where the grantee contributed or participated in the conception or reduction to practice of such new use;

    (b) Where the patent would hamper, impede, or infringe on the intended use of the invention;[1]

---

[1] Agreement, as revised in December 1966, eliminates these criteria.

(c) Where the new use is within the field of research work supported by the grant.[1]

(iv) The government shall receive a nonexclusive, irrevocable, royalty-free license to any new use patent and shall also have the power to sub-license others for all governmental purposes.

The drug firms almost unanimously rejected the amended patent agreement from the beginning for several reasons:

(i) They refused to accept the loss of prospective proprietary rights.

(ii) They feared the contamination[2] of in-house research that would result from taking in compounds arising from NIH-sponsored research.

(iii) They thought that they might lose control over the testing and the reporting of results.

The immediate effect of the drug firms' refusal to sign the amended patent agreement was their almost complete withdrawal from screening compounds resulting from NIH-sponsored research. However, the overall effects of the policy on the interactions necessary for successful completion of the drug development process are much broader.

The nearly complete blockage of testing—an essential step in the utilization of compounds conceived or developed under NIH sponsorship—is an obvious major effect of HEW patent policy in effect prior to late 1966. The almost total refusal of drug firms to screen (and subsequently develop) these compounds created an insurmountable obstacle to their ultimate utilization, except possibly in those areas (cancer and malaria) where the government operates its own screening services.[3]

What is not so obvious but equally important is the second major effect of patent policy in this area: The crippling limitations on the necessary flow of ideas

---

[1] Agreement, as revised in December 1966, eliminates these criteria.

[2] As used by the drug industry and university investigators, "contamination" means the potential compromise of rights in proprietary research resulting from exposure of an individual or organization to ideas, compounds, and/or test results arising from government-sponsored research. For example, a compound developed under NIH-sponsored research comes into a drug firm for screening and is found to be useful in a therapeutic area in which the company has conducted prior research; the company incorporates into its research program some of the research findings from the screening of the NIH compound, and the company then develops a marketable product. The company is afraid that HEW is in a position to assert claims to that product. Figures issued by the Pharmaceutical Manufacturers Association show that the drug industry supports the greatest research and development effort per sales dollar (8.7 percent of sales in 1964) of any industry class.

[3] In 1967 approximately 55 agreements were signed by three firms under the revised patent agreement form adopted in December 1966.

---

among the groups that must participate in the drug development process if it is to be successful. This interference occurs even earlier in the drug development process and has even broader impact than the blockage that results from the refusal of the drug firms to screen NIH-sponsored compounds.

2. The Two Major Effects

Before the promulgation in 1962 of the new procedures for HEW patent policy administration, the interplay between the academic community and the drug industry was concrete and specific. A drug firm could actually work, in pursuit of its own interests, with a professor's compound; the professor received, in return, not only the kind of testing appropriate to his specific intentions and test data sufficient for publication, but also, in many cases, practical suggestions about continuation of his research, new avenues of investigation, and, sometimes, the opportunity to pursue further work under specific industrial research grants. The free pharmacological advice and counsel to which the academic medicinal chemist often had access was of the most practical and experienced type available anywhere. At the same time, the relationship between the academic investigator and the drug firm allowed for recycling—based upon test results—of the research. Positive test results from the drug firm could be incorporated readily into the investigator's research design for further work, and he was almost always assured of the availability of additional testing.

When the drug firms stopped testing compounds conceived or developed under NIH sponsorship, the investigators developing these compounds had to turn to other sources of testing—government, university, and independent testing laboratories. The advantages and disadvantages of these respective sources of testing can be summarized as follows:

- *Government Testing Laboratories*
  Although some attempt may be made by the two government laboratories—Cancer Chemotherapy National Service Center (CCNSC) and Walter Reed Army Institute of Research (WRAIR)—to accommodate the specific intentions of the academic investigator who developed the compound being screened, the high volume of tests usually precludes all but the most standardized screening for activity against the two disease systems, cancer and malaria. For example, although potentially analgesic, antihistaminic, or other compounds may be submitted to CCNSC or to WRAIR for testing on the outside chance that they may show activity (and often merely to allow the academic investigators to

publish that the compounds have at least been tested for something), the compounds most likely will not be tested for their intended—and potentially most effective—uses.

● *University Testing Laboratories*

University-run laboratories have only limited capability to carry out pharmacological evaluation beyond the first gross qualitative steps. In most cases, they have limited access to professional pharmacologists, no experience with FDA requirements and procedures, and little interest in active compounds beyond finding out why they are active.

● *Independent Testing Laboratories*

Both types of independent testing laboratories—commercial and nonprofit—that evaluate academically prepared compounds must charge for their services so that their testing is self-supporting.[4] Although some of the independent testing laboratories can offer a rather complete line of pharmacological testing capabilities, costs tend to be beyond the scope of the academic investigators' grant budgets. Representatives of one independent testing laboratory, an organization capable of performing a fairly complete range of services for academic investigators, said that there have been only a handful of tests performed for principal investigators in the 15 or so years of the organization's experience, and that the total value of all of this work would not exceed $10,000. They attributed the low volume to the costs that they had to charge in order to earn a profit from testing. In some cases, nonprofit organizations may have grants that allow them to run specific screens; however, this is not true in all medically interesting areas.

It does not seem to matter much which screening source other than drug firms is used to test the NIH-sponsored compounds—the result is the same (except in the case of a compound that proves useful in treating cancer or malaria.)[5] Having to do without the

drug firms' screening services—which in their total range include specific screening, extensive test results, and concomitant development work—means to the academic investigator that the work on his compound that is necessary for ultimate utilization is cut off, in most cases, at the development stage.

The second major effect of current government patent policy is the serious weakening of the communications links vital for the productive interchange of research ideas. Prior to 1962, the interchange of ideas among the NIH, university investigators, professional journals, and drug firms was accomplished through consulting relationships, work on compounds, test data, and papers. Since 1962, two of these media for interchange of ideas—the flow of compounds and investigators—have been virtually eliminated. The other two media—consulting relationships and papers—have been diluted by the lack of drug industry screening services for NIH-sponsored compounds. Drug firms currently seem to screen their consultants carefully; a criterion for an acceptable consultant seems to be noninvolvement with government research related to the drug firm's interests. With regard to papers, the lack of extensive—or even, in many cases, specific—test results has led to decreased publication of results of medicinal chemistry research. In addition, two media contacts through scientific seminars and personal friendships have been affected to some extent.

In summary, many extremely important contacts among academic, industrial, and government researchers in areas outside of cancer and malaria have been either eliminated or seriously decreased because of the current patent policy and the consequent threat of "contamination" of industrial research. In contrast, when the compound originates under a drug industry grant, the working relationship between the academic investigator and the drug firm screening his compound is very close, and research can be recycled or replanned as necessary to meet specific goals.

From their respective testing services outlined above, the roles and operating patterns of the various screening sources can be summarized as follows. The pharmacology department of a drug firm acts as a sort of sophisticated broker between an inventory of tens of thousands of compounds (some generated by academic investigators and some generated through in-house efforts) and the clinical requirements of the medical profession. Since it is specifically oriented to cancer and malaria, the pharmacology work done by CCNSC and WRAIR also falls in this category. The pharmacology department of a university probably functions more as a scientific knowledge-gathering organization operating with an inventory of compounds and producing state-

---

[4] In contrast, testing by a pharmaceutical firm is essentially a by-product of its need for research, testing by government agencies is funded because of important national goals, and testing within universities is squeezed out of operating budgets by interested faculty members.

[5] Because of the large amounts of money available for cancer research and malaria research, the availability of testing facilities in these fields, and the fact that compounds in these fields seem to have the greatest chance for utilization, cancer research and malaria research are attracting great interest and effort on the part of university investigators in medicinal chemistry. Compounds found, through government screening, to be useful in treating cancer or malaria are developed by the government and can be carried through the remainder of the drug development process to the consumer.

of-the-art studies. Commercial testing organizations are less broadly focused than either the pharmacology department of a drug firm or the pharmacology department of a university. The operations of a non-profit testing organization can resemble the operations of any of the other screening sources, depending on the specific circumstances of the nonprofit organization.

With regard to the second effect of patent policy—the limitation on productive interchange of research ideas—practically every scientist interviewed in this study was worried about the comparative isolation of academic and government investigators from their drug industry counterparts. Vital communications links have been weakened in large measure by the problem of "contamination." Drug firms are negative about government patent policy not so much because they may lose rights to the outside compounds that they test, but because the outside compounds, any related in-house items that they may already have, and any and all ideas submitted to them by academic investigators may become the subject of a claim of rights by the Surgeon General. Consequently, drug firms are quite concerned about keeping all ideas that may have come from NIH-sponsored research segregated from their own research. To accomplish this segregation, they have minimized those professional contacts and meetings that could later be construed as having contributed to their own research.

The issue of contamination of ideas arises with regard to several other sources of ideas in addition to the NIH idea itself. Was the research that the journal article described performed under an NIH grant? Did the colleague communicate ideas developed under NIH sponsorship? Because of the investigator's intimate knowledge of NIH-projects, can virtually anything he does be considered contaminated? The implications of these questions are worrying the drug industry.

The implications of government patent policy do not end with the proposal preparation phase—the typical investigator is continually confronted with patent questions while pursuing his projects. For example,

consider the case of an investigator with an industry-sponsored project, a foundation-sponsored project, and an NIH-sponsored project. He reads professional literature, attends meetings, and keeps up his contacts in his search for new ideas and approaches. In addition, his own analysis and experimentation on each project yield data that may have application to his other projects and to projects of his professional associates within his organization. He must continually live with the question of the extent to which he must recognize proprietary and government patent rights—and with the adverse effects that appropriate recognition of these rights necessarily has upon what would otherwise be relatively free research communications. For the diligent respecter of rights, current government patent policy tends to inhibit contacts among associates and the concomitant idea flow between projects and to prevent the results of work sponsored by NIH from being used in further drug research.

Evidence that the effects observed in the medicinal chemistry program were not just an isolated occurrence in one industry was found in cases relating to development of two biomedical inventions. In both instances, companies with investments in private research and portfolios of background patents to products similar to those the government was proposing to develop, hesitated to deal with NIH if they had to forego title to inventions developed under government contract or give up rights to related background patents. Similar experiences were encountered in Department of Interior programs, as reported in Volume II of the study. Although there was insufficient data to determine how broadly government programs are affected by nonparticipation of industry for patent reasons, it seems clear that some programs are. To deal with these problems as they surface, it may be desirable to establish a procedure that provides for reexamination of their treatment under the policy when a government agency finds that the policy is materially affecting accomplishment of a program.

Appendix B: Presidential Memorandum, August 23, 1971

THE WHITE HOUSE
WASHINGTON

August 23, 1971

MEMORANDUM FOR HEADS OF EXECUTIVE
DEPARTMENTS AND AGENCIES

On October 10, 1963, President Kennedy forwarded to the Heads of Executive Departments and Agencies a Memorandum and Statement of Government Patent Policy for their guidance in determining the disposition of rights to inventions made under Government-sponsored grants and contracts. On the basis of the knowledge and experience then available, this Statement first established Government-wide objectives and criteria, within existing legislative constraints, for the allocation of rights to inventions between the Government and its contractors.

It was recognized that actual experience under the Policy could indicate the need for revision or modification. Accordingly, a Patent Advisory Panel was established under the Federal Council for Science and Technology for the purpose of assisting the agencies in implementing the Policy, acquiring data on the agencies' operations under the Policy, and making recommendations regarding the utilization of Government-owned patents. In December 1965, the Federal Council established the Committee on Government Patent Policy to assess how this Policy was working in practice, and to acquire and analyze additional information that could contribute to the reaffirmation or modification of the Policy.

The efforts of both the Committee and the Panel have provided increased knowledge of the effects of Government patent policy on the public interest. More specifically, the studies and experience over the past seven years have indicated that:

(a) A single presumption of ownership of patent rights to Government-sponsored inventions either in the Government or in its contractors is not a satisfactory basis for Government patent policy, and that a flexible, Government-wide policy best serves the public interest;

(b) The commercial utilization of Government-sponsored inventions, the participation of industry in Government research and development programs, and commercial competition can be influenced by the following factors: the mission of the contracting agency; the purpose and nature of the contract; the commercial applicability and market potential of the invention; the extent to which the invention is developed by the contracting agency; the promotional activities of the contracting agency; the commercial orientation of the contractor and the extent of his privately financed research in the related technology; and the size, nature and research orientation of the pertinent industry;

(c) In general, the above factors are reflected in the basic principles of the 1963 Presidential Policy Statement.

Based on the results of the studies and experience gained under the 1963 Policy Statement certain improvements in the Policy have been recommended which would provide (1) agency heads with additional authority to permit contractors to obtain greater rights to inventions where necessary to achieve utilization or where equitable circumstances would justify such allocation of rights, (2) additional guidance to the agencies in promoting the utilization of Government-sponsored inventions, (3) clarification of the rights of States and municipal governments in inventions in which the Federal Government acquires a license, and (4) a more definitive data base for evaluating the administration and effectiveness of the Policy and the feasibility and desirability of further refinement or modification of the Policy.

I have approved the above recommendations and have attached a revised Statement of Government Patent Policy for your guidance. As with the 1963 Policy Statement, the Federal Council shall make a continuing effort to record, monitor, and evaluate the effects of this Policy Statement. A Committee on Government Patent Policy, operating under the aegis of the Federal Council for Science and Technology, shall assist the Federal Council in these matters.

This memorandum and statement of policy shall be published in the Federal Register.

Richard Nixon

Attachment

Statement of Government Patent Policy

Basic Considerations

A. The Government expends large sums for the conduct of research and development which results in a considerable number of inventions and discoveries.

B. The inventions in scientific and technological fields resulting from work performed under Government contracts constitute a valuable national resource.

C. The use and practice of these inventions and discoveries should stimulate inventors, meet the needs of the Government, recognize the equities of the contractor, and serve the public interest.

D. The public interest in a dynamic and efficient economy requires that efforts be made to encourage the expeditious development and civilian use of these inventions. Both the need for incentives to draw forth private initiatives to this end, and the need to promote healthy competition in industry must be weighed in the disposition of patent rights under Government contracts. Where exclusive rights are acquired by the contractor, he remains subject to the provisions of the antitrust laws.

E. The public interest is also served by sharing of benefits of Government-financed research and development with foreign countries to a degree consistent with our international programs and with the objectives of U.S. foreign policy.

F. There is growing importance attaching to the acquisition of foreign patent rights in furtherance of the interests of U.S. industry and the Government.

G. The prudent administration of Government research and development calls for a Government-wide policy on the disposition of inventions made under Government contracts reflecting common principles and objectives, to the extent consistent with the missions of the respective agencies. The policy must recognize the need for flexibility to accommodate special situations.

Policy

Section 1. The following basic policy is established for all Government agencies with respect to inventions or discoveries made in the course of or under any contract of any Government agency, subject to specific statutes governing the disposition of patent rights of certain Government agencies.

(a) Where

(1) a principal purpose of the contract is to create, develop or improve products, processes, or methods which are intended for commercial use (or which are otherwise intended to be made available for use) by the general public at home or abroad, or which will be required for such use by governmental regulations; or

(2) a principal purpose of the contract is for exploration into fields which directly concern the public health, public safety, or public welfare; or

(3) the contract is in a field of science or technology in which there has been little significant experience outside of work funded by the Government, or where the Government has been the principal developer of the field, and the acquisition of exclusive rights at the time of contracting might confer on the contractor a preferred or dominant position; or

(4) the services of the contractor are

(i) for the operation of a Government-owned research or production facility; or

(ii) for coordinating and directing the work of others,

the Government shall normally acquire or reserve the right to acquire the principal or exclusive rights throughout the world in and to any inventions made in the course of or under the contract.

In exceptional circumstances the contractor may acquire greater rights than a nonexclusive license at the time of contracting where the head of the department or agency certifies that such action will best serve the public interest. Greater rights may also be acquired by the contractor after the invention has been identified where the head of the department or agency determines that the acquisition of such greater rights is consistent with the intent of this Section 1(a) and is either a necessary incentive to call forth private risk capital and expense to bring the invention to the point of practical application or that the Government's contribution to the invention is small compared to that of the contractor. Where an identified invention made in the course of or under the contract is not a primary object of the contract, greater rights may also be acquired by the contractor under the criteria of Section 1(c).

(b) In other situations, where the purpose of the contract is to build upon existing knowledge or technology, to develop information, products, processes, or methods for use by the Government, and the work called for by the contract is in a field of technology in which the contractor has acquired technical competence (demonstrated by factors such as know-how, experience, and patent position) directly related to an area in which the contractor has an established nongovernmental commercial position, the contractor shall normally acquire the principal or exclusive rights throughout the world in and to any resulting inventions.

(c) Where the commercial interests of the contractor are not sufficiently established to be covered by the criteria specified in Section 1(b) above, the determination of rights shall be made by the agency after the invention has been identified, in a manner deemed most likely to serve the public interest as expressed in this policy statement, taking particularly into account the intentions of the contractor to bring the invention to the point of commercial application and the guidelines of Section 1(a) hereof, provided that the agency may prescribe by regulation special situations where the public interest in the availability of the inventions would best be served by permitting the contractor to acquire at the time of contracting greater rights than a nonexclusive license.

(d) In the situations specified in Sections 1(b) and 1(c), when two or more potential contractors are judged to have presented proposals of equivalent merit, willingness to grant the Government principal or exclusive rights in resulting inventions will be an additional factor in the evaluation of the proposals.

(e) Where the principal or exclusive rights in an invention remain in the contractor, he should agree to provide written reports at reasonable intervals, when requested by the Government, on the commercial use that is being made or is intended to be made of inventions made under Government contracts.

(f) Where the principal or exclusive rights in an invention remain in the contractor, unless the contractor, his licensee, or his assignee has taken effective steps within three years after a patent issues on the invention to bring the invention to the point of practical application or has made the invention available for licensing royalty-free or on terms that are reasonable in the circumstances, or can show cause why he should retain the principal or exclusive rights for a further period of time, the Government shall have the right to require the granting of a nonexclusive or exclusive license to a responsible applicant(s) on terms that are reasonable under the circumstances.

(g) Where the principal or exclusive rights to an invention are acquired by the contractor, the Government shall have the right to require the granting of a nonexclusive or exclusive license to a responsible applicant(s) on terms that are reasonable in the circumstances (i) to the extent that the invention is required for public use by governmental regulations, or (ii) as may be necessary to fulfill health or safety needs, or (iii) for other public purposes stipulated in the contract.

(h) Whenever the principal or exclusive rights in an invention remain in the contractor, the Government shall normally acquire, in addition to the rights set forth in Sections 1(e), 1(f), and 1(g),

(1) at least a nonexclusive, nontransferable, paid-up license to make, use, and sell the invention throughout the world by or on behalf of the Government of the United States (including any Government agency) and States and domestic municipal governments, unless the agency head determines that it would not be in the public interest to acquire the license for the States and domestic municipal governments; and

(2) The right to sublicense any foreign government pursuant to any existing or future treaty or agreement if the agency head determines it would be in the national interest to acquire this right; and

(3) the principal or exclusive rights to the invention in any country in which the contractor does not elect to secure a patent.

(i) Whenever the principal or exclusive rights in an invention are acquired by the Government, there may be reserved to the contractor a revocable or irrevocable nonexclusive royalty-free license for the practice of the invention throughout the world; an agency may reserve the right to revoke such license so that it might grant an exclusive license when it determines that some degree of exclusivity may be necessary to encourage further development and commercialization of the invention. Where the Government has a right to acquire the principal or exclusive rights to an invention and does not elect to secure a patent in a foreign country, the Government may permit the contractor to acquire such rights in any foreign country in which he elects to secure a patent, subject to the Government's rights set forth in Section 1(h).

Section 2. Under regulations prescribed by the Administrator of General Services, Government-owned patents shall be made available and the technological advances covered thereby brought into being in the shortest time possible through dedication or licensing, either exclusive or nonexclusive, and shall be listed in official Government publications or otherwise.

Section 3. The Federal Council for Science and Technology in consultation with the Department of Justice shall prepare at least annually a report concerning the effectiveness of this policy, including recommendations for revision or modification as necessary in light of the practices and determinations of the agencies in the disposition of patent rights under their contracts. The Federal Council for Science and Technology shall continue to:

(a) develop by mutual consultation and coordination with the agencies common guidelines for the implementation of this policy, consistent with existing statutes, and to provide overall guidance as to disposition of inventions and patents in which the Government has any right or interest; and

(b) acquire data from the Government agencies on the disposition of patent rights to inventions resulting from federally financed research and development and on the use and practice of such inventions to serve as bases for policy review and development; and

(c) make recommendations for advancing the use and exploitation of Government-owned domestic and foreign patents.

Each agency shall record the basis for its action with respect to inventions and appropriate contracts under this statement.

Section 4. Definitions: As used in this policy statement, the stated terms in singular and plural are defined as follows for the purposes hereof:

(a) *Government agency:* includes any executive department, independent commission, board, office, agency, administration, authority, Government corporation, or other Government establishment of the executive branch of the Government of the United States of America.

(b) *States:* means the States of the United States, the District of Columbia, Puerto Rico, the Virgin Islands, American Samoa, Guam and the Trust Territory of the Pacific Islands.

(c) *Invention, or Invention or discovery:* includes any art, machine, manufacture, design, or composition of matter, or any new and useful improvement thereof, or any variety of plant, which is or may be patentable under the Patent Laws of the United States of America or any foreign country.

(d) *Contractor:* means any individual, partnership, public or private corporation, association, institution, or other entity which is a party to the contract.

(e) *Contract:* means any actual or proposed contract, agreement, grant, or other arrangement, or subcontract entered into with or for the benefit of the Government where a purpose of the contract is the conduct of experimental, developmental, or research work.

(f) *Made:* when used in relation to any invention or discovery means the conception or first actual reduction to practice of such invention in the course of or under the contract.

(g) *To the point of practical application:* means to manufacture in the case of a composition or product, to practice in the case of a process, or to operate in the case of a machine and under such conditions as to establish that the invention is being worked and that its benefits are reasonably accessible to the public.

Appendix C: Current Statutes, Regulations, Orders, Manuals, Memorandums, and Materials Governing Allocation of Rights to Inventions Arising from Government-Sponsored Research

I. Government Employment Inventions

Rights to inventions made by government employees, except for those of the Atomic Energy Commission, are determined by the provisions of:

A. Exec. Order No. 10,096 (January 23, 1950), 15 Fed. Reg. 389, 3 C.F.R. 1949 53, Comp., as amended by Exec. Order No. 10,930 (March 24, 1961), 26 Fed. Reg. 2583, 3 C.F.R. 1969-63, Comp., as implemented by 27 Fed. Reg. 3289 (April 6, 1962), 37 C.F.R. 100 (1962).

B. Exec. Order No. 9365 (June 14, 1947), 12 Fed. Reg. 3907, 37 C.F.R. 101, 102.

Many federal departments and agencies have regulations which spell out the administrative procedures of 37 C.F.R. 100, 101, 102.

II. Contractor Inventions

Rights to inventions arising from government-sponsored R&D are determined by statute and/or under contract provisions pursuant to the August 1971 Presidential Memorandum and Statement of Government Patent Policy (Appendix B). The following is a list of federal departments and agencies with citations and references pertaining to their respective patent policies. Paragraph F identifies the office primarily responsible for patent matters. The list of regulations includes those reported to the Federal Council for Science and Technology on December 31, 1972, and those believed to have been issued prior to December 31, 1973.

The format and material for this appendix were taken, in part, from the *Annual Report on Government Patent Policy* of the Federal Council for Science and Technology.

List of Departments and Agencies Cited

Cabinet Departments

Department of Agriculture
Department of Commerce
  National Technical Information Service
Department of Defense
Department of Health, Education, and Welfare
Department of Housing and Urban Development
Department of the Interior
Department of Justice
  Law Enforcement Assistance
  Administration
Department of Transportation
Department of the Treasury

Independent Agencies

Arms Control and Disarmament Agency
Atomic Energy Commission
Central Intelligence Agency
Environmental Protection Agency
Federal Communications Commission
National Aeronautics and Space Administration
National Science Foundation
Postal Service
Tennessee Valley Authority
Veterans Administration

Cabinet Departments

Department of Agriculture

A. *Statutory Authority*

- Research and Marketing Act of 1946, Pub. L. No. 79-733, 60 Stat. 1085 and 1090, 7 U.S.C. 4271 and 1624 respectively.

B. *Regulations*

- Title 7, §185d of the Administrative Regulations of the U.S. Department of Agriculture (pertains to cooperative agreements).

- Agricultural Procurement Regulations, tit. 41, C.F.R., Subpt. 4-3.51, Negotiated Research Agreements with Educational Institutions, particularly §4-3.5105(c)(2).

- 41 C.F.R. 4-16.5200(a)(1), Forms for Research Agreements.

C. *Other*

- Form AD-451 (March 1971), Research Agreements.

- Form AD-452 (March 1971), General Provisions for Research Agreements, particularly §17.

- Form AD-455 (March 1971), Guidelines for Research Agreements, Pub. L. No. 85-934 and Pub. L. No. 89-196, particularly §II, Administration of Research Grants, Patents. (Forms AD-452 and 455 were originally published on August 7, 1970, 35 Fed. Reg. 12607.)

D. *Informal Literature*

- None.

E. *Presidential Policy Statement*

- Consult Chief, Research Agreements and Patent Management Branch, Administrative Services Division, Hyattsville, Maryland 20782.

F. *Office Primarily Responsible for Patent Matters*

- Mr. Rubin Hoffman, Deputy Director (Patents), Research and Operations Division, Office of General Counsel, Department of Agriculture, Washington, D.C. 20250. Phone: 202-477-5474.

Department of Commerce

A. *Statutory Authority*

- None.

B. *Regulations*

- Department of Commerce Department Administrative Order 202-735A, "Employee Responsibilities and Conduct," §3, "Employee Inventions"

(November 5, 1969), and Department Administrative Order 208-14, "Department of Commerce Patent Policy for Contracts and Grants" (October 18, 1967): 32 Fed. Reg. 15890 (November 18, 1967).

C. *Other*

- National Bureau of Standards Administrative Manual, Ch. 2, Subch. 10 (April 30, 1968), "Employee Inventions"; Maritime Administration Administrator's Order 205, amended (November 10, 1967), "Employee Inventions."

D. *Informal Literature*

- None.

E. *Presidential Policy Statement*

- Department Administrative Order 208-14 fully implements the Presidential Policy Statement.

F. *Office Primarily Responsible for*
Patent Matters

- Mr. David Robbins, Patent Advisor, National Bureau of Standards, Room A419, Administration Building, Washington, D.C. 20234. Phone: 301-921-3412.

Department of Commerce
National Technical Information Service

A. *Statutory Authority*

- None.

B. *Regulations*

- The NTIS is charged with the commercial utilization of government-held patents.

C. *Other*

- The NTIS publishes a weekly bulletin, *Government Inventions for Licensing*, pursuant to GSA licensing regulations.

D. *Informal Literature*

- The NTIS issues regular publications on patents and data available to industry.

E. *Presidential Policy Statement*

- See Department of Commerce.

F. *Office Primarily Responsible for Patent Matters*

- Mr. Douglas Champion, Patent Advisor, National Technical Information Service, Springfield, Virginia. Phone: 703-451-6556.

Department of Defense

A. *Statutory Authority*

- None.

B. *Regulations*

- Armed Services Procurement Regulation (ASPR), §9-107, §9-109, and §18-903; 32 C.F.R. 9.107-3, 9.109, 9.202-2, 9.301-2, and 18-908. (The Defense Department issues revisions of ASPR from time to time which appear in the daily *Federal Register*.)

C. *Other*

- Defense Procurement Circular No. 65, dated December 20, 1968. (This circular lists the educational or nonprofit institutions with approved patent policies permitting the use of the license clause at the time of contracting in certain circumstances.)

D. *Informal Literature*

- None.

E. *Presidential Policy Statement*

- The Presidential Policy Statement is substantially printed verbatim in ASPR.

F. *Office Primarily Responsible for*
   Patent Matters

- Mr. Walter Henderson, Procurement Analyst, Directorate for Procurement Policy, OASD (I&L), Department of Defense, Room 3D776, Pentagon, Washington, D.C. 20301. Phone: 202-OX7-7076.

- Lt. Col. James E. Noble, Chief, Patents Division, Office of The Judge Advocate General, Department of the Army, Washington, D.C. 20310. Phone: 202-OX5-6822.

- Capt. Frank S. Johnston, Assistant Chief for Patents, Office of Naval Research, Department of the Navy, Arlington, Virginia 22217. Phone: 202-OX2-4000.

- Mr. Harry A. Herbert, Jr., Chief, Patents Division, Office of The Judge Advocate General, Department of the Air Force, Washington, D.C. 20314. Phone: 202-OX3-5710.

Department of Health, Education, and Welfare

A. *Statutory Authority*

- Solid Waste Disposal Act, Pub. L. No. 89-272, tit. II S202(c), 79 Stat. 997, 42 U.S.C. S3253(c).

B. *Regulations*

- 31 Fed. Reg. 12842 (October 1, 1966), 45 C.F.R. subtit. A, Pts. 6 and 8.

C. *Other*

- HEW General Administration Manual, Pt. 6, Patents and Inventions, Chs. 6-10, Regulations and Procedures; HEW Organization Manual, Pt. 1, General Ch. 1-901, Department Patent Activities; HEW Procurement Manual Circular HEW-66, Patent Rights Cl. 20 of HEW General Provisions; PHS Policy Statement—Grants for Research, Projects, PHS Publication No. 1301. The Secretary of Health, Education, and Welfare has approved a standard form of Institutional Patent Agreement for use in conjunction with Pt. 8, §8.1(b) of the HEW General Administration Manual.

D. *Informal Literature*

- None.

E. *Presidential Policy Statement*

- Regulations were not specifically rewritten following the issuance of the October 1963 Presidential Policy Statement since they were considered to be in conformity thereto.

F. *Office Primarily Responsible for Patent Matters*

- Mr. Norman J. Latker, Chief, Patent Branch, Department of Health, Education, and Welfare, Room 5A03, Westwood Building, Bethesda, Maryland 20014. Phone: 301-496-7056.

Department of Housing and Urban Development

A. *Statutory Authority*

- None.

B. *Regulations*

- None.

C. *Other*

- Patents clause for HUD procurement contracts.

D. *Informal Literature*

- None.

E. *Presidential Policy Statement*

- Policy of this Statement is implemented through HUD's patents clause for procurement contracts.

F. *Office Primarily Responsible for Patent Matters*

- Mr. William L. Johncox, Administrative Law Branch, Office of General Counsel, Department of Housing and Urban Development, Washington, D.C. 20510. Phone: 202-755-7137.

Department of the Interior

A. *Statutory Authority*

- Coal Research Act of July 7, 1960, §6, Pub. L. No. 86-599, 74 Stat. 337, 30 U.S.C. 666 (1964).

- Helium Act Amendments of September 13, 1960, §4, Pub. L. No. 86-777, 74 Stat. 920, 50 U.S.C. 167b (1964).

- Saline Water Conversion Act of September 22, 1961 §4b, Pub. L. No. 87-295, 75 Stat. 628, 42 U.S.C. 1954b (1964).

- Water Resources Research Act of July 17, 1964, Pub. L. No. 88-379, 78 Stat. 330, 42 U.S.C. 1961c-3 (1964).

- Appalachian Regional Development Act of March 9, 1965, Pub. L. No. 89-4, as amended, 79 Stat. 5, as amended, 40 App. U.S.C. 302(e) (1964 Supp. V).

- Solid Waste Disposal Act of October 20, 1965, Pub. L. No. 89-272, 79 Stat. 997, 42 U.S.C. 3253(c) (1964 Supp. V).

- Federal Coal Mines Health and Safety Act of 1969, Pub. L. No. 91-173, 83 Stat. 742, tit. V, §501(c).

B. *Regulations*

- Regulations implementing the Presidential Policy Statement are being drafted. 43 C.F.R. Pt. 6, Patent Regulations: Subpt. A covers inventions made by employees; Subpt. B covers patent licensing. 41 C.F.R. 14 R-9, Patents and Data Clauses for Office of Saline Water R&D Contracts and Grants.

C. *Other*

- Department of the Interior Departmental Manual, Pt. 453, Ch. 2 (August 1969), "Inventions by Contractors' Employees."

D. *Informal Literature*

- Solicitor's Memorandum Opinion M-36637, "Patent Requirements of the Coal Research Act, Saline Water Conversion Act and Helium Act," 69 I.D. 54(1962).

E. *Presidential Policy Statement*

- Unless governed by statutory requirements, the policy of this Statement is followed.

F. *Office Primarily Responsible for Patent Matters*

- Mr. Frank A. Lukasik, Assistant Solicitor, Branch of Patents, Department of the Interior, Washington, D.C. 20240. Phone: 202-343-4471.

Department of Justice
Law Enforcement Assistance Administration

A. *Statutory Authority*

- Omnibus Crime Control and Safe Streets Act of 1968, Pub. L. No. 90-351, 83 Stat. 197. As amended, Pub. L. No. 91-644, 84 Stat. 1881.

B. *Regulations*

- In preparation.

C. *Other*

- None.

D. *Informal Literature*

- Financial Guide, General Conditions Applicable to Administration of Grants Under Pt. C and Pt. E of tit. I, Pub. L. No. 90-351, as amended by tit. I, Pub. L. No. 91-644. Form LEAA-OLEP-5-1-7 (November 18, 1970), Application for Grant/Discretionary Funds, Grant Conditions (2) and (3).

E. *Presidential Policy Statement*

- Determination with respect to the administration and disposition of title to and rights in inventions and patents thereon are governed by the criteria of the Presidential Policy Statement.

F. *Office Primarily Responsible for Patent Matters*

- Mr. Thomas Madden, General Counsel, Law Enforcement Assistance Administration, Department of Justice, 633 Indiana Avenue NW., Washington, D.C. 20530. Phone: 202-386-3333.

Department of Transportation

A. *Statutory Authority*

- §106(c) of the National Traffic and Motor Vehicle Safety Act of 1966, 80 Stat. 721, 15 U.S.C. 1395(c), applies to certain contracts and grants of the National Highway Traffic Safety Administration, Department of Transportation (DOT). Section 307 of tit. 23, U.S.C., applies to the Federal Highway Administration, DOT.

B. *Regulations*

- 41 C.F.R. 12, Department of Transportation Procurement Regulation (DOTPR), Pt. 12-9, Patents, Data, Copyrights, and Recovery of Developmental Costs. These regulations were published on February 11, 1972 (37 Fed. Reg. 4802), and became effective throughout DOT on June 2, 1972. Before that date, each of the operating administrations had its own regulations or none at all.

C. *Other*

- DOT Order No. 2100.3 Employee Inventions.

D. *Informal Literature*

- None.

E. *Presidential Policy Statement*

- The Statement of Government Patent Policy, which is set forth verbatim in DOTPR 12-9.6191, is followed.

F. *Office Primarily Responsible for*
   Patent Matters

- Mr. Nathan Edelberg, Patent Counsel, Office of the General Counsel, Department of Transportation, 400 Seventh Street SW., Washington, D.C. 20590. Phone: 202-426-9738.

Department of the Treasury

A. *Statutory Authority*

- None.

B. *Regulations*

- None.

C. *Other*

- None.

D. *Informal Literature*

- None.

E. *Presidential Policy Statement*

- Policy of this Statement is followed.

F. *Office Primarily Responsible for*
Patent Matters

- Mr. Forest D. Montgomery, Chief, Opinions Section, Office of the General Counsel, Department of the Treasury, Washington, D.C. 20220. Phone: 202-964-5311.

Independent Agencies

Arms Control and Disarmament Agency

A. *Statutory Authority*

- Arms Control Disarmament Act, §32, 22 U.S.C. 2572.

B. *Regulations*

- 41 C.F.R. 23-52.1, 41 C.F.R. §§23-50.403.

C. *Other*

- None.

D. *Informal Literature*

- None.

E. *Presidential Policy Statement*

- Agency policy and regulations take account of the Presidential Policy Statement and the specific requirements of the statute that established ACDA (see A above).

F. *Office Primarily Responsible for Patent Matters*

- Mr. William W. Hancock, General Counsel, U.S. Arms Control and Disarmament Agency, Washington, D.C. 20451. Phone: 202-632-3708.

Atomic Energy Commission

A. *Statutory Authority*

- Atomic Energy Act of 1954, Pub. L. No. 83-703, 68 Stat. 919, 42 U.S.C. 2011-2281 (Patents and Inventions, 2181-2190, as amended).

B. *Regulations*

- Procurement Regulations, Pt. 9-9, Patents and Copyrights, 41 C.F.R. 9-9 (revised annually) (originally published 29 Fed. Reg. 17113, December 15, 1964, minor revisions since published in Fed. Reg. are incorporated in 41 C.F.R. 9-9 with Fed. Reg. references), C.C.H. 3 Atomic Energy Law Reports, Par. 15,606.

- Pt. 9-7, Contract Clauses, 9-7.5006-13, Drawings, Designs, Specifications, 41 C.F.R. 9-7.5006-13, 25 Fed. Reg. 8870 (September 15, 1960), C.C.H. 3 Atomic Energy Law Reports, Par. 15,606.

C. *Other*

- Policy as to licensing of AEC-owned domestic and foreign patents. TID 4557 (3rd Rev.) (August 1969); Pt. 81, 10 C.F.R. 38 Fed. Reg. 7318; and 38 Fed. Reg. 8216.

- Compensation or Awards Under §157 of the Atomic Energy Act of 1954, as amended, Pt. 80, 10 C.F.R.

- Rights in Data and Inventions in Contractor Independent Research and Development, AECPR §9-9.5019 and §9-15.5010-12, 33 Fed. Reg. 228 (November 22, 1968).

D. *Informal Literature*

- R.A. Anderson, Atomic Energy Patents, "The Encyclopedia of Patent Practice and Invention Management," Calvert, Reinhold (1964).

E. *Presidential Policy Statement*

- Policy of this Statement is used in conjunction with the statutory authority (see B above).

F. *Office Primarily Responsible for*
Patent Matters

- Mr. Roland A. Anderson, Assistant General Counsel for Patents, U.S. Atomic Energy Commission, Washington, D.C. 20545. Phone: 301-973-5162.

Central Intelligence Agency

A. through E.

- Agency follows the regulations of the Department of Defense in all patent matters.

F. *Office Primarily Responsible for*
Patent Matters

- Mr. Oliver E. Pagan, Associate General Counsel, Central Intelligence Agency, Room 1206, Ames Center Building, Washington, D.C. 20505. Phone: 703-351-2565.

Environmental Protection Agency

A. *Statutory Authority*

- Solid Wastes Disposal Act, Pub. L. No. 89-272, as amended by the Resources Recovery Act, Pub. L. No. 91-512, 42 U.S.C. 3253(c).

B. *Regulations*

- Interim grant regulations published, 36 Fed. Reg. 229 (November 27, 1971). Went into use January 1, 1972.

- Proposed contract regulations published for rule making in V. 37 Fed. Reg. 35 (February 19, 1972).

- All regulations constitute an implementation of the President's Patent Policy Statement of August 21, 1971 (Fed. Reg., August 26, 1971).

C. *Other*

- In all grants awarded after January 1, 1972, the regulations referred to in B, above, are used. In contracts, EPA is using patent clauses used by the Department of the Interior and the Department of Health, Education, and Welfare, respectively, since these clauses were being used by components of EPA which were formerly in said departments. As indicated above, a single patent clause for the entire agency is being drafted.

D. *Informal Literature*

- None.

E. *Presidential Policy Statement*

- Policy of this Statement is followed.

F. *Office Primarily Responsible for Patent Matters*

- Mr. Benjamin H. Bochenek, Patent Counsel, Division of Grants and Procurement, Office of General Counsel, Environmental Protection Agency, Washington, D.C. 20460. Phone: 202-755-0794.

Federal Communications Commission

A. *Statutory Authority*

- None.

B. *Regulations*

- None.

C. *Other*

- None.

D. *Informal Literature*

- None.

E. *Presidential Policy Statement*

- Policy of this Statement is followed.

F. *Office Primarily Responsible for Patent Matters*

- Mr. Chester D. Roberts, Jr., Assistant General Counsel, Federal Communications Commission, 1919 M Street NW., Washington, D.C. 20554. Phone: 202-632-6947.

National Aeronautics and Space Administration

A. *Statutory Authority*

- National Aeronautics and Space Act of 1958, Pub. L. No. 85-568, 72 Stat. 435, 42 U.S.C. 2457.

B. *Regulations*

- Patent Waiver Regulations (May 28, 1966), 31 Fed. Reg. 7677-7679, 14 C.F.R. 1245.1.

- Patent Licensing Regulations (October 26, 1962), 27 Fed. Reg. 10446-10448, 14 C.F.R. 1245.2.

- Foreign Patent Program (February 10, 1965), 30 Fed. Reg. 1844, 14 C.F.R. 1245.3.

- Foreign Patent Licensing Regulations (August 18, 1966), 31 Fed. Reg. 10958-10959, 14 C.F.R. 1245.4.

- NASA Procurement Regulations, Pt. 9: Innovations, Inventions, Patents, Data and Copyrights (March 1970).

C. *Other*

- *Awards for Inventions*

    −NASA Management Issuance NMI 1152.17A (August 2, 1967), "NASA Inventions and Contributions Board," 32 Fed. Reg. 11209-11210 (August 2, 1967), 14 C.F.R. 1209.4.

—NASA Management Issuance NMI 5700.1 (June 22, 1967), "Awards for Scientific and Technical Contributions," 32 Fed. Reg. 6272-6273 (April 21, 1967), 14 C.F.R. 1240.1.

—NASA Policy Directive NPD 5700.2A (December 14, 1968), "Policy on Awards for Reported Technical and Scientific Contributions—NASA and Contractor Employees."

—NASA Management Issuance NMI 5700.3A (December 14, 1968), "Procedures for Making Awards for Reported Technical and Scientific Contributions—NASA and Contractor Employees."

- NASA Hand Book NHB 2170.1 (October 1966), "Management Guidelines for New Technology Reporting to NASA."

- NASA Hand Book NHB 2170.3 (April 1969), "Documentation Guidelines for New Technology Reporting."

- NASA Hand Book NHB 5500.1A (February 1966) (Change 7), "Findings of Fact and Recommendations of the NASA Inventions and Contributions Board."

- Significant Patent Forms Used by Agency: NASA Form 554—Instrument of Waiver; NASA form 1317—Petition for Waiver Under §1245.104 or .105 of the NASA Patent Waiver Regulations; NASA Form 1318—Petition for Waiver under §1245.106 of the NASA Patent Waiver Regulations; NASA Form 1162—New Technology Clause for Contracts; NASA Form 1135—Nonexclusive Revocable License for Patent; NASA Form 1136—Nonexclusive Revocable License for Patent Application; NASA Form 1137—Power to Inspect and Make Copies (of Licensed Application for Patent); NASA Form 66A—New Technology Report; NASA Form 1393—Patent Waiver Report; NASA Form 1427—Patent License Report.

D. *Informal Literature*

- None.

E. *Presidential Policy Statement*

- Regulations implement the Presidential Policy Statement in their compliance with the statutory authority.

F. *Office Primarily Responsible for Patent Matters*

- Mr. Leonard Rawicz, Assistant General Counsel for Patent Matters, National Aeronautics and Space Administration, 400 Maryland Avenue SW., Washington, D.C. 20546. Phone: 202-755-3932.

National Science Foundation

A. *Statutory Authority*

- National Science Foundation Act of 1950, Pub. L. No. 81-507, 76 Stat. 1253, 42 U.S.C. 1870(c) and 1871(a).

B. *Regulations*

- NSF is presently in the process of drafting patent regulations further implementing the Policy Statement.

C. *Other*

- NSF Circular No. 71 (Revision No. 1) (August 7, 1970), "Disposition of Rights in Inventions Made in the Course of Activities Supported by NSF"; NSF 73-26, Grant Administration Manual, issued October 1973, setting forth interim regulations on patents and inventions in §251, 242.

D. *Informal Literature*

- Staff Memorandum O/D 65-20 (October 18, 1965), "Revised Patent Policy"—Attachments.

E. *Presidential Policy Statement*

- The Grant Administration Manual identified in C implements the Presidential Policy Statement.

F. *Office Primarily Responsible for*
Patent Matters

- Mr. William J. Hoff, General Counsel, National Science Foundation, Washington, D.C. 20550. Phone: 202-632-4386.

Postal Service

A. *Statutory Authority*

- None.

B. *Regulations*

- None.

C. *Other*

- None.

D. *Informal Literature*

- None.

E. *Presidential Policy Statement*

- The criteria of this Statement is followed by the Service.

F. *Office Primarily Responsible for Patent Matters*

- Mr. Luther A. Marsh, Patent Counsel, Contracts and Property Division, U.S. Postal Service, 12th & Pennsylvania Avenue NW., Washington, D.C. 20260. Phone: 202-961-6130.

Tennessee Valley Authority

A. *Statutory Authority*

- Tennesee Valley Authority Act of 1933, as amended §5(i), Pub. L. No. 73-17, 48 Stat. 58, 61, 16 U.S.C. §831, 831d(i).

B. *Regulations*

- None.

C. *Other*

- TVA Code, Office of the General Manager II Inventions, 1-3 (April 13, 1972).

D. *Informal Literature*

- None.

E. *Presidential Policy Statement*

- Policy of this Statement is observed. See reference in TVA Code in C above.

F. *Office Primarily Responsible for*
Patent Matters

- Mr. L. Duane Dunlap, Assistant General Counsel, Tennessee Valley Authority, Knoxville, Tennessee 37902. Phone: 615-637-0101, Ext. 2522.

Veterans Administration

A. *Statutory Authority*

- None.

B. *Regulations*

- VA Regulations 650-663, 38 C.F.R. 1.650-1.663.

C. *Other*

- None.

D. *Informal Literature*

- None.

E. *Presidential Policy Statement*

- Policy of this Statement is followed.

F. *Office Primarily Responsible for*
Patent Matters

- Mr. John J. Corcoran, General Counsel, Veterans Administration, Washington, D.C. 20420. Phone: 202-DU9-3831.

Notes

Notes

Chapter 1
Study Objectives

1. It is not an overstatement to say that the really significant problems in the law of intellectual property affecting utilization today are at the interstices of the various legal disciplines rather than in, say, patents or trade secrets per se.

Chapter 2
Summary of Findings

1. The 1968 study was concerned exclusively with government-sponsored research. Most of the organizations in the present study did very little, if any, government contracting.

2. The Arkwright textile mill trade secret was stolen in 1769 by Samuel Slater, an apprentice in Great Britain who memorized the equipment and brought the industrial revolution to America.

Chapter 3
Legal Parameters

1. But see B.F. Skinner, who argues in *Beyond Freedom and Dignity* that the distinction between the carrot and the stick is a semantic illusion.

2. *Report of the President's Commission on the Patent System* (1966), p. 2.

3. *Kewanee Oil v. Bicron*, 94 S. Ct. 1879 (1974). The Supreme Court by a six-to-two decision reversed a ruling of the 6th circuit that federal patent law preempts the use of trade secrets for patentable subject matter. The case is discussed more fully in Chapter 7.

4. See Chapter 7, Trade Secret and Industrial Know-How.

5. See DOD Instruction 5010.12.

Chapter 4
Research Methodology

1. The ubiquitous suppression of literature, which is the major subject of copyright law, is not included within the scope of the study. See footnote 2.

2. The inadequacies of copyright law have led to universally acknowledged adverse commercial consequences which definitely affect downstream marketing

of technology if not "utilization" as defined here. Information technology regularly outstrips the development of copyright law. It took Congress almost 50 years to amend the copyright law so that it would apply to phonograph records. It has yet to begin to come to grips with the interaction of xerography and tape recorders with the "fair-use" doctrine. Thus, there is scarcely a major book publisher in the country who cannot point to some manuscript which remains unpublished because anticipated circulation would be too small to compete with unauthorized reproductions, or some record publisher who has not been hurt by bootleg tapes.

Chapter 5
Breaking the Barriers

1. *Fortnightly Corp. v. United Artists Television*, 88 S. Ct. 2084 (1968) [hereinafter cited as *Fortnightly*].

2. *Use of the Carterfone Device in Message Toll Telephone Service*, 13 F.C.C. 2d 420 (1968) [hereinafter cited as *Carterfone*].

3. *Fortnightly* supra note 1, at 2091.

4. Ibid.

5. Ibid.

6. The "legislative solution" is still pending.

7. *Carterfone*, supra note 2.

8. 14 F.C.C. 2d 571 (1968).

9. See Figure 1-1.

10. Here the shaded area represents the relation of these cases to the scope of the entire study.

Chapter 6
Patents

1. See, generally, Toulmin, *Patents and the Antitrust Laws*, and articles cited in the 1973 pocket part to Chapter 8.

2. As will be noted in the intellectual property survey sample discussed in Chapter 7, the industry tends to include many small businesses.

3. A note, *Patent Pooling and the Sherman Act*, 50 Colum. L. Rev. 1113 (1950), holds that the criteria used by the courts to determine the legality of patent pools are the dominant position of the parties and their intent.

4. In one interview a high company official conceded that emission control is not a matter of technology but rather of what the market is willing to pay.

5. The public position of the industry is to the contrary. For example, Ford reported to its stockholders that from 1967 to 1972 it spent $360 million on

research to reduce emissions and to that end, almost exclusively, employed 3,000 scientists, engineers, technicians, and support personnel. It had also filed 122 patent applications in the field, of which 57 had been allowed at the time of the interview (November 1973).

6. See Appendix B.

7. See Appendix C.

8. *Public Citizen, Inc. v. Sampson*   F Supp   (U.S.D.C., Dist. of Columbia, January 19, 1974).

9. The principal fear of the title proponents is that discretionary government licensing practices may strengthen monopoly and reduce competition. The principal fear of the license proponents is that government-sponsored research might not be utilized because of inadequate investment incentive in the absence of exclusive rights. The 1968 study was able to uncover only a single instance (in the small synthetic quartz industry) in which government patent policy created a monopoly. It uncovered many more instances in which companies such as oil and pharmaceutical firms (which did not need government rights to strengthen their market positions) simply refused to engage in government contracting.

10. A patent license may be exclusive as to (1) use, (2) manufacture, and (3) sale. The patent owner may grant a license that is exclusively territorial or exclusive as to certain types of articles manufactured under the license. Licensing contracts, which traditionally include royalty inspection and litigation provisions, may be used to unreasonably restrain trade in violation of antitrust laws. In an address to the American Patent Law Association on October 11, 1973, Karl E. Bakke, General Counsel of the U.S. Department of Commerce, said that "the Department of Commerce will continue to monitor developments concerning the relationship between patent licensing and the antitrust laws. If specific supporting data becomes available establishing that the value of the patent grant is being diminished through court decisions applying general antitrust principles to the specialized area of licensing practices, we most certainly will support corrective legislation."

11. Copies of correspondence from May 22 to July 9, 1973, are in project files.

12. "Nonprofit" is a broad classification. The reference here is to institutions like the Woods Hole Oceanographic Institute, which is an East Coast counterpart to the Scripps Institute of Oceanography in La Jolla, California. The only principal structural difference between the two is that Scripps is part of the University of California and Woods Hole is an independent "nonprofit" institution. The term "nonprofit" would not include firms such as Mitre Corporation and Aerospace Corporation, which are also nonprofit but whose operations are closer to industrial application than to academic theory. These two companies are also government laboratory surrogates to specific federal agencies. See Miller, "Legal Organization of Research-Based Industry," 41 B.U. Law Rev. 69 (1961).

13. In the 1968 Government Patent Policy Study, Harbridge House examined the practices of 67 representative institutions.

14. The one-year grace period of the Patent Code of 1952 would be preserved by the administration's Patent Modernization and Reform Act of 1973 as well as by S.1321 and S.1975, the opposition patent reform bills introduced in 1973. From time to time patent reform bills have proposed bringing the U.S. patent system in line with those of other countries which have eliminated patent interferences by adopting a first-to-file policy. If the grace period were ever eliminated, the universities would then have to choose between publishing *or* patenting, a choice in which utilization would be the loser.

Chapter 7
Trade Secret and Industrial Know-How

1. ALI Restatement of the Law of Torts, §757.

2. See Trade Secrets and the Roman Law, 30 Colum. L. Rev. 837 (1930).

3. See Tom Arnold and Jack C. Goldstein, "Painton v. Bourns, The Progeny of Lear v. Adkins: A Commentary on Know-How Law and Practice," *Trade Secrets Today* (Practising Law Institute, 1971).

4. See Roger M. Milgrim, *Trade Secrets* (New York, Matthew Bender & Company, Incorporated, 1973).

5. *Telex Corp. v. IBM*, No. 72-C-18, No. 72-C-89 (D.N. Ore., filed September 17, 1973).

6. 395 U.S. 653, 89 S. Ct. 1902 (1969).

7. 309 F. Supp. 271 (S.D.N.Y.), rev'd, 442 F(2) 216 (2d in 1971).

8. In addition to *Painton*, which was the most recent case on the subject, other courts that refused to declare a conflict between federal patent law and state trade secret law include the Fourth Circuit in *Servo Corporation of America v. General Electric Co.*, 337 F. 2d 716; the Ninth Circuit in *Dekar Industries, Inc., v. Bissett-Berman Corp.*, 434 F. 2d 1304; and the Fifth Circuit in *Water Services, Inc., v. Tesco Chemicals, Inc.*, 410 F.2d 163.

9. Op. cit. chap. 3, n. 3 at p. 1888.

10. The written questionnaires were circulated with the support of the PTC Research Foundation (Franklin Pierce Law Center), formerly the Patent, Trademark & Copyright Institute of George Washington University.

11. An extensive study of patent licensing practices in the United States, sponsored by the French government, has recently been concluded by M. Alain Anizon of the Centre d'Etudes Economiques d'Entreprises. After 10 months of interviewing government and private licensing executives in this country, M. Anizon mentioned to the Harbridge House project staff, one of his most surprising findings was the total lack of communication among resident or retired patent attorneys, licensing executives, and marketing personnel in American industry.

12. However, it should be noted that Exxon, one of the petroleum-group participants in the survey, widely advertises an offer of royalty-free licenses to the "bottom-tension boom" device for containing offshore oil spills.

13. See Armed Services Procurement Regulation 9-202.

14. 15 U.S.C. §46(d).

15. *Covey Oil Co. v. Continental Oil Co.*, 340F. 2d 933, 999 (10th Cir. 1965).

16. 18 U.S.C. §1905.

17. No. 8884 FTC (October 2, 1973).

18. It must be conceded that an original recipe bears a marked similarity to a secret chemical process.

19. Quoted by Hummerstone, "How the Patent System Mousetraps Inventors," *Fortune* (May 1973), p. 262.

Chapter 8
Copyright and Data

1. From the Patent Act of 1793 to the Patent Act of 1836.

2. IBM's 1969 announcement that it would price separately from hardware most new computer programs and most systems engineering and educational services.

3. Gottschalk v. Benson, 93 S. Ct. 253 (1972).

4. In the opinion of the Copyright Office, there is a question whether a computer program fits the statutory definition for copyrightable material. However, in accordance with its policy of resolving doubtful questions in favor of registration, it accepts computer programs as long as certain formalities are observed.

5. Correlations were made using the "rank-difference" technique.

6. The attention of the reader is invited to the correlation between this finding and the nearly identical finding in the intellectual property survey in Chapter 7.

7. All patent applications would be published for opposition under the 1973 Patent Reform Bill.

8. *Public Citizen v. Sampson,* _____ F. Supp. _____ (U.S.D.C., Dist. of Columbia, January 19, 1974).

9. Each of NASA's own field centers has a patent attorney and a technology utilization officer.

10. The regional application centers are located at the University of Connecticut, Indiana University, University of Pittsburgh, University of Southern California, Research Triangle Park in North Carolina, and the University of New Mexico.

11. There is often considerable ambiguity regarding copyright ownership. An

interesting example is the paperback book *Records, Computers, and the Rights of Citizens*, which is published by Massachusetts Institute of Technology with a copyright legend and sells for $2.45. The identical book (from the same reproducible master, but lacking a second foreword by Elliot Richardson and with a different cover) is sold by the GPO for $2.

12. *"Report to the Committee on Scientific and Technical Information of the Federal Council on Science and Technology from Its Panel on Legal Aspects of Information Systems," The Honeywell Computer Journal* 7, no. 1 (1973). Also available from NTIS, Springfield, Virginia, as COSATI 73-01.

Index

Index

About the Author

Richard I. Miller is an authority on the integration of problems of law, science, and business administration. He is a Principal of Harbridge House, Inc., a multinational management consulting firm, and has published and lectured on a variety of related topics ranging from the legal organization of research-based industry to problems of computer privacy. He received the B.A. in the philosophy of science from the University of California at Berkeley in 1950 and the J.D. from Yale University Law School in 1953; subsequently, he pursued post-professional studies at Harvard University Law School.